VOLUME 1

SUPERHERO SUCCESS™

Endorsed by Don Green,

Executive Director of

The Napoleon Hill Foundation

This book is for:

_____

because I believe you are a Superhero, and I care about you!

YOUR NEXT BREAKTHROUGH... IS ONLY ONE DECISION AWAY!

— Praise For TW Walker's Superhero Success —

"I read Superhero Success and was amazed at the valuable information that was made available through the storyline. I recommend you read this book, and take the story and apply it in your life for a better future."

Don M. Green
Executive Director, The Napoleon Hill Foundation
Author, Everything I Learned About Success I Learned From Napoleon Hill

---

"I couldn't put it down! The imagination; the pure brilliance of wrapping such a valuable life and business lesson in a story like this! You are a Superhero, Mr. Walker!"

Walter Bergeron
GKIC Marketer of the Year
Author - *The Million Dollar Total Business Transformation*

"One thing I know about getting to your Next Level is that you will have challenges along the way and it will require (not request) the ability to breakthrough those in order to get there. Superhero Success is written in such a way that anyone can identify with, learn from and gain the courage to become a true superhero for their friends, their family, their community and most importantly, to the themselves!"

Bob Donnell
CEO | Next Level Live
Live At Your Next Level

— Praise For TW Walker's Superhero Success —

"In all my years of reading self help and motivational type books, Superhero Success gets to the core of what holds people back from true success-FEAR! This book will surly be read, even studied, by anyone wanting to know, and understand more about overcoming negative thoughts. Superhero Success will teach you the fundamental basics of having what you think and say. This book will inspire you, in a fun and exciting way, to reach deep inside yourself for inner strength and courage, so that you, too, will have 'Superhero Success' in every area of your life."

Daniel M. Stephens
Publisher | CEO, Who's Who Magazines, Inc.

"Part business leader and part adventure hunter, TW Walker just created a one-of-a-kind story about building character, fostering leadership qualities and overcoming the fear that holds most of us back from obtaining true riches in our personal and professional lives.

Superhero Success is a must-read for those entrepreneurial souls looking to laugh and discover an adventure through the eyes of a young child. The journey, which takes flight with an 8-year-old boy who is dead set on becoming a Superhero, is a testament to perseverance - offering many life lessons that should be modeled and respected by young and old alike."

Kendra Jo Murphy
Copywriter and Multi-Step Marketing Strategist

"This is an absolute must-read! Superhero Success, in all its comic book simplicity, provides a formula for success all fathers should share with their children. TW Walker takes a creative, unique and most importantly, smart approach to leadership and performance that resonates for not only adults, but for the younger generation as well. Don't allow yourself or your children to slip into mediocrity. By studying this book together, you will not only strengthen your relationship with your children, but you'll uncover and unleash the Superhero powers that are within each of us."

Matt Patterson
Author of Amazon Best Seller, *My Emily*

— Praise For TW Walker's Superhero Success —

"Great for all ages, this fun, fast and insightful story will have you on the edge of your seat as you follow the characters along the roadmap to achieving success... like a Superhero!"

Dr. Danny Brassell
America's Leading Reading Ambassador
Founder of The Lazy Readers' Book Club

"This is a great book for anyone looking to make improvements in their lives; and who isn't? Well-written in a way to not only assists the reader in gaining valuable insight in how to reach professional and personal success, but also in an entertaining way. The lessons found in this book will help each reader become successful by teaching them how to harness the power of their mind to reach their goals. A valuable tool for today's fast-paced and tough times."

Bradley Sniderman
Attorney
Los Angeles, CA

For more information, contact Breakthrough Media Network.

Copyright © 2015 by Breakthrough Media Network
All rights reserved.

Published by Breakthrough Media Network

15 Paradise Plaza, Ste. 272
Sarasota, FL 34239
www.TWWalker.com

Superhero Success™, CAPE-ability®, Captain Breakthrough®, and Fear Sucks® are trademarks owned by Breakthrough Media Network. All trademarks and pending trademarks are property of their rightful owner.

Printed in the United States of America.

Editorial consultant: Heather O'Brien Walker
Illustration contributor: Miranda Mundt

Printed in the United States of America

ISBN: 978-0-9855393-0-6

SUPERHERO SUCCESS ™

Expand Your CAPE-ability® To Break Through Any Challenge, Overcome Any Fear, And Accomplish Any Goal!

A Superhero is more than a comic representation of a super human "being"...it's a metaphor of power within the common vulnerabilities, weaknesses, and fears we all deal with at some level. This fun and simple parable is great for people of all ages to learn how to overcome fears that debilitate growth on the road to success.

BECOME A SUPERHERO IN LIFE AND BUSINESS!

by TW Walker

ARE YOU READY TO STRAP ON YOUR CAPE?

— Acknowledgments —

First and foremost, I'd like to thank Don Green of the **Napoleon Hill foundation for the endorsement and support of my work.** I think it's awesome what the organization stands for and hope it continues for generations to come as more and more people embrace the invaluable lessons Dr. Hill taught that continue to live on decades after his death.

With appreciation words could never do justice, I'd like to also to thank my wife, Heather. You helped me with every aspect of this book, and also supported me throughout this and every other crazy adventure I wanted to take you on since I've known you. The world really does need more people with the sincerity, kindness, and love you display to me on a daily basis.

I'd also like to give thanks to my mom and dad, Chuck and Diana Walker. I cannot remember a single instance where you both have not been there to support every outlandish or crazy idea I've ever had. I have so many fond memories of you both and appreciate your constant love and encouragement.

Lastly, I'd like to thank the long list of friends, colleagues, mentors, and confidants I've met, known, and studied over the years that have helped me persevere on my own journey.

— Dedication —

With all the gratitude my Superhero body can muster, I dedicate this book to one and only one person: my wife, Heather.

You said I was nuts to accept the challenge, but I did it anyway.

You trusted me and embraced my dream with me, even though I knew nothing about writing and publishing a book. Even though we were planning a wedding and moving, you stood behind me.

Without you, I would never have been able to complete this book on a crazy, self-imposed deadline. Through several weeks of writing, re-writing, editing, brainstorming, and collaborating (and a lot of wine and laughs in between) we've proven to the world that a darn good book can be written and published when you set your mind to it.

You are the quintessential team player. You are the ultimate partner and I'm proud to call you my wife.

I love you. You are my twin flame…you are my Superhero. In fact, you are my SuperSHEro.

— Warning! —

Don't let the simplicity and "comic strip come to life" style of this book fool you. There are very powerful lessons within the story you are about to read. Lessons based on Napoloen Hill's world famous Law Of Success told as a parable with interesting twists.

If you're experiencing dissatisfaction, confusion, or fear in any aspect of your life, then get ready to find clarity, focus, and fearlessness by learning the secrets of Superhero Success™. When you apply the strategies presented in this book, and consistently follow them, you will discover the magic of sleeping powers that exist within you right now. The powers of a Superhero within you.

You may not be living the life you have always wanted consciously. You may be trying to figure out what you want to pursue in life. You may have even started a business that you want to take to the next level, or are thinking about starting one. Perhaps you have a hobby or passion, and you want to turn that into your primary income. Many people fall into one or more of those categories, and from that point, they get stuck or experience what's commonly known as "spinning your wheels". Think you know the secrets of how to achieve success? Well think again.

As an accomplished entrepreneur, I've witnessed just about every aspect of failure and success. Based on my years of experience and diligent study of human behavior, fear, and mind control, I have discovered that nothing works like a positive mindset and organized plan toward attaining a very distinct goal. This, along with taking consistent action steps and precise implementation, is the only way to live a life of your own design and keep fear from controlling you.

A Superhero, as I've come to define it in very general terms, is someone who is positively and passionately pursuing a worthwhile goal. There are many other facets to living the life of a Superhero, and it's for this very reason that living the life of a Superhero is not for everyone. Becoming and maintaining the life of a Superhero can best be described as being one amongst many. It is a life fraught with overcoming huge obstacles, breaking through mind-numbing challenges, and dealing with the many faces and the incessant presence of fear.

If you're ready to achieve Superhero Success™ then get ready to strap on your cape and soar to new heights!

— Foreword —

"Success is simple, but definitely not easy. TW Walker has taken the simple principles of success and presented them in a clever, fun way in which we watch "Captain Breakthrough" battle the ever-present "Dr. Fear". It's a challenge that we all must overcome on our rise to achieving our dreams.

TW has overcome those roadblocks in his own life, and in the process, has definitely become a Superhero of Success. He is changing the world, and invites you to join him. You will enjoy the wisdom and inspiration contained in this motivational comic book, as you "break through any challenge, overcome any fear, and accomplish any goal!"

Scott Alexander
Author of *Rhinoceros Success*

Scott self-published his book in 1980 at the age of 23, and now, going into its fourth decade of popularity, he's sold over 3,000,000 copies. The popularity of his first book led to others in the series:

- *Advanced Rhinocerology*
- *Rhinocerotic Relativity*

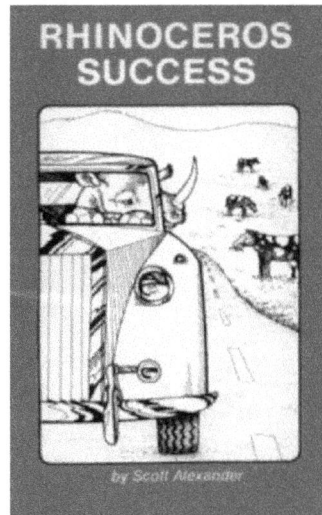

RHINOCEROS SUCCESS

by Scott Alexander

– Preface –

Throughout this delightful story, you will understand the "child within us all" attitude you need to become a Superhero in your own life and business. Use it to remind yourself that such a quest requires hard work, dedication and desire. With the awesome super powers of thought, persistence, a positive mindset, and perseverance you are destined to reach Superhero Success™.

When we're born, we all have two basic fears: fear of falling and fear of loud noises. According to Dr. Napoleon Hill, fear is considered to be the number one cause of failure in unsuccessful people. To make matters worse, we're already born completely dependent on others for *all* our necessities. The bad news is that fear can easily strengthen as we go through life. The good news is that it can also be minimized to the point of being virtually non-existent if you learn and implement the laws of success as first taught by Napoleon Hill decades ago.

So what's the difference? Why do we humans have a tendency to fear more and more as we get older and experience more of life? Simple. In a nutshell, it's because of failure and rejection. Worse is the fact that it's the failure and rejection of *others* that's freely projected on you that plants the seed of doubt or worry that causes the fear in the first place. Usually, it's from the people closest to us, and that's because they, too, have experienced failure and rejection in their own lives and think they're actually doing you a favor by telling you to be realistic, to go the safe route, etc. And so the trend continues to perpetuate throughout life. Only a mere few ever learn how to conquer fear and keep it contained in order to maintain positivity, and achieve in life.

Also according to Dr. Napoleon Hill, there are six core human fears that, at some level, affect us all, but each of these fears, referred to in the book as "villains", also have comrades they work closely with. If you're going to experience success at high levels, then you must learn how to strategically plant your own seeds [goals], then tend that mental garden daily. What is it that you want? How badly do you want it? If you plant the right seeds, and you nurture those seeds carefully every day, then the universe will respond. No different than if you planted an actual seed into a garden. When nurtured with care, it will produce a healthy harvest.

If not nurtured with care, however, the garden will quickly be filled with weeds and eventually the weeds will prevail. The weeds are the fear, doubt, worry, stress, procrastination, and more. With training, you will easily be able to break through fears that restrict growth, encourage inaction, hold you back, promote negativity, and more…but you also must learn how to manage fear and its many comrades.

This is not an easy task, and it's often one that is completely overlooked and avoided. As with the garden example, all too often, people think that if they simply plant a seed, if they plant a seed at all, it will mysteriously grow into a fruitful and robust garden. Fear is something that, if not dealt with head-on, will grow and become more powerful. It will rear its ugly head in every aspect of your life, unless controlled. Although there are many valuable lessons throughout the book, dealing with fear and its comrades are the core lessons found in Superhero Success™.

Fearful are those who have lost their sense of hope and let their dreams shrivel up and go dormant, without knowing that the seed of it was still alive and well-hidden in the recesses of their conscious minds. I know that everyone, at some time in their life, probably during childhood, wished that they had some kind *superpower or* wondered what it would be like to fly. This is the seedling from which the entire premise for the book came about. For me, I wanted more than anything to fly and, in my mind, I believed that I could.

As a result, I have always pictured myself as a Superhero wearing a cape— due to my infatuation with the one and only, Superman. I admired him and his powerful ways; flying faster than a speeding bullet or leaping tall buildings. But, what I also saw was that he still had something in his life that made him merely mortal, or simply human. As if to imply that we all have his potential lying dormant within us.

So knowing that the seeds of belief, hope, and big dreams are somewhere within us all – the Superhero within – just imagine all that undiscovered, untapped, potential lying dormant within you. Perhaps due to the influence of outside negativity, or not knowing how to access that super potential, you have gotten sidetracked on your path to Superhero Success™.

Those who felt there was a Superhero within when you were a child, and even those who know there still is, will hopefully allow that Superhero to soar again after reading this book. Once you break free from the chains of fear that have been holding you back, you'll be able to overcome any obstacle in your life.

If the desire for success is present in your conscious mind, you will draw upon a properly programmed unconscious to become that Superhero. Those powers will provide enough motivation and more inspiration to take you to the next level of "Superherodom", and you will be well on your way to being the ferocious, speeding, powerful, unstoppable super force to be reckoned with.

Once you've implemented the principles in this book, you'll be flying at warp speed with laser beam focus. You'll find yourself tearing through anything and everything in your path, on your way to Superhero Success™, the home of the happy Superhero. There you will be living a life of your own design, not one of default.

Keep in mind however that success is ultimately a journey, not a destination. And as one ancient Chinese Proverb states:

"The journey of a thousand miles begins with a single step." I like to say "The journey of a thousand miles begins with a CAPE."

Either way, it's imperative that you enjoy yourself along the way. Regardless of your age, hopefully you will find inspiration from this story to take your inner super powers all the way to the Superhero Success™ you've always wanted.

At any point, fear or one of its many comrades may take a strangle hold on you. Remember, it's ultimately your choice how long you choose to let them keep you in that position. You can let it stay the same, or you can break free from the grasp, but it takes effort, and sometimes there may be a mental struggle. Until the pain of being fearful and scared is greater than the pain of breaking through it to succeed and live an abundant lifestyle by strategic design, then fear will always have the upper hand on you.

So as you read the book, let your mind go back to that fearless child within you that's unafraid to dream big and be adventurous. Just for a moment, imagine what your world would look like with anything at all being possible, that anything you can imagine and believe with all your heart can be yours. You see, once you've learned how to strap on your proverbial cape, you will begin to expand your CAPE-ability® and achieve magnificent things in your life.

TW Walker

"FEARS ARE NOTHING MORE THAN A STATE OF MIND."
- DR. NAPOLEON HILL

— Prologue —

In this charming and entertaining parable, a comic strip that's come to life, based on Napoleon Hill's world famous laws of success, you'll learn how a savvy father harnesses the mind of his wildly imaginative young son, Gordy, to teach him the fundamental laws of success. With the help of his son's favorite Superhero, Captain Breakthrough, Gordy's dad finds unique ways to help his son attain success as a kid, and even later, as an adult.

The world of fantasy unfolds as Captain Breakthrough plunges onto the scene as a Superhero representation of everything success embodies. Being a newly certified Superhero, he still has much to learn and, in some instances, he, too, can succumb to the power of his nemesis, the evil Dr. Fear. Captain Breakthrough quickly realizes that a positive mental attitude is the most effective weapon he has to thwart the efforts of his foe, so he constructs a "PMA" Shield and employs this weapon, among others, to engage in the battle.

At the opposite end of the spectrum, Dr. Fear is the embodiment of everything that fear represents. His weapons are doubt, worry, stress, failure, hopelessness and low self-esteem, and he concocts a diabolical scheme to fill people's minds with fear so that he can control the world.

Then there's Gordy's dad, a successful motivational author and speaker, who recognizes Gordy's fascination with the Captain Breakthrough cartoon. Every week, he watches his young son's fascination with the show grow, so he takes the opportunity to ingrain the laws of success into his son's mind by crafting analogies from the events unfolding on the television screen. He coins the term Superhero Success™, so it will make more sense to his young son.

Gordy is a very intelligent, quick-witted eight-year-old who chooses to happily live in his head, where his version of Captain Breakthrough takes on "other worldly" dimensions. Along with his loyal dog, Jack, Gordy lives in his own Superhero world. Through his dad, Gordy learns what it takes to be a

Superhero and achieve Superhero Success™ with each passing day.

Finally, Gordy has become a man living the life he has designed for himself. He has followed in his father's footsteps and he himself is a successful author and motivational speaker, passing on the message of Superhero Success™ he learned from his dad. From his adult perspective, Gordy reflects back on his days as a fearless eight year old learning the laws of success from Captain Breakthrough and his father.

Gordy and his cartoon characters will demonstrate, perhaps, what you have forgotten, by taking you back to those innocent days of your childhood, while the relationship he has with his dad will teach and inspire you to Superhero Success.

Now, strap on your cape, throw it back over your shoulders, and join Gordy as he embarks on his mission to become Captain Breakthrough and annihilate Dr. Fear!

— Table Of Contents —

— Chapter 1 —
Thinking Like A Superhero

Pride gleamed from his eyes as the thick, silky, blue cape was carefully draped around his neck. Although relatively heavy, even for a man of his stature, it felt light in comparison to how big he felt at that moment. Chest was out, arms were back, lips were firm, and a smile formed on his face. He was now officially licensed and qualified as a Superhero.

The years of preliminary work and study at the Superhero Academy were over - now the real work would begin. He had people to save, and more importantly, a reputation to build. In more than seven years of intense physical and mental work, he had learned many valuable lessons, and he knew that this cape signified more than just an education; it represented much more about life.

His mind began to imagine all the places he would soar, all the people he would help, and all the influence he would have on the world. He even imagined the busts and statues that someday would be erected in his honor, yet at this point, he did not yet fully realize what was happening in his mind. He was growing.

Then it dawned on him that he needed a name, a moniker.

"What can I call myself?" the dashing young man quietly asked aloud. And no sooner had the question sounded from his mouth, than the answer became clear in his mind.

"I've overcome so many obstacles and challenges over the last seven years," he said to himself, confidently.

"In fact, I didn't just OVERCOME them, I broke THROUGH them!" he continued. After a slight pause, he uttered to himself.

"I'm Captain Breakthrough..." and then he paused again, obviously still deep in thought. Then, like a light turning on, he exclaimed:

"That's IT!! I AM CAPTAIN BREAKTHROUGH!" he roared.

"And I'm going to SAVE the people of the world from fear, and help them overcome the obstacles of life, so they can succeed in whatever they set out to do!" Once he said it out loud, the reality of his declaration hit him. It was real.

The confidence brimmed from his face, and he knew his future, his CALLING, his chief aim in life, was now determined. He could feel his desire for greatness burning inside him like a white hot flame. He wanted nothing more than to become a global icon of help for the few people of the world who chose to truly embrace success.

He had learned at the Academy that fear was very powerful. He knew that it could completely consume someone…even paralyze them…if they didn't know how to identify its presence, and take the appropriate steps to control it.

Although he didn't realize it at the moment, Captain Breakthrough was about to embark on a life journey that would define his entire career, his entire life. Captain Breakthrough was indeed going to become a global icon, but the journey would not be easy.

Far away, in places where Captain Breakthrough had not yet ventured, trouble was brewing. Shrouds of darkness were starting to descend, and the atmosphere was becoming heavy. He began to hear rumors of this strange phenomenon, but had no idea that it was fear itself. Fear had been festering, untreated for so long, that it had captured one man's heart, and consumed him to the point where he had developed inexplicable powers. Unbeknownst to Breakthrough, his name was Dr. Fear.

Although Captain Breakthrough's confidence was high, he knew that in order to truly master his craft, he had much more work to do. Otherwise, he would remain vulnerable to fear and negativity.

"It's all about the attitude," he thought to himself.

"In fact, it's all about having a positive mental attitude," he clarified. And with those words, the seed of an idea for a shield from all negativity was planted.

After toiling in his private mountain lair workshop for several weeks, Breakthrough's Positive Mental Attitude (PMA) shield was ready for action. Or so he thought. Even though he was brimming with confidence, he couldn't help but wonder, *Is a positive mental attitude enough to power this*

SUPERHERO ACADEMY

shield against fear?

What Captain Breakthrough didn't know at that point was that his brimming confidence would be the catalyst that would carry him through the many obstacles and challenges he would face on his journey toward ultimate success. He didn't know what he didn't know, but he was determined to learn. He knew what he wanted to accomplish, and that nothing would stand in his way of helping people around the world achieve their life goals by overcoming their fears.

Weeks later, while Breakthrough was immersed in learning everything he could about his new profession, he read the glaring headline on the front page of the local newspaper:

"Dr. Fear To Control The World!"

Alarmed and concerned, he had a hunch that this had something to do with the shroud of darkness he'd been hearing so much about. After reading the entire article, Captain Breakthrough leapt to his feet and exclaimed.

"This is it! This is my chance to hit the big time…I will defeat fear on a global level!" He flipped on his high frequency negativity scanner to determine specifically where the havoc was taking place. Once the location was locked, preparation was underway.

He strapped on his cape, attached his PMA shield to his muscular right arm, and took off like a blue streak into the air. At warp speed, Breakthrough arrived on the scene, but he wasn't prepared for what he saw. This was going to be the biggest challenge of his life.

Fear had grown so strong amongst the people, and was spreading so fast, that it had become an epidemic of vast proportions. Everyone seemed to be in a state of panic and despair, the likes of which Captain Breakthrough had never witnessed before. He could see it in their grief-stricken eyes.

"What's happening here?!" Breakthrough gasped aloud to himself.

What would have normally been a serene and orderly main street of any small town was now a chaotic and disturbing scene. Men were

shouting at each other, women were screaming, children were crying, and local businesses were being looted. The police were trying frantically to manage the situation.

Although Breakthrough could not 'see' him, he knew that Dr. Fear was present. For the first time, Captain Breakthrough felt the true gravity of the situation. Dr. Fear would soon destroy the world if Breakthrough didn't intervene in a big way.

Using sheer determination, Breakthrough commanded the people's attention, and snapped them out of their induced state of negativity. He quickly instilled calmness and positivity in the people with a motivational speech of encouragement:

"Your thoughts will make or break you . . . thoughts always come first. Guard them closely. You can do ANYTHING you want to do in life, but it all starts with your thinking! Success is a mindset!" he bellowed.

Incredibly, Captain Breakthrough's words seemed to cut through the people's trance-like states, and the panic slowly lifted. After temporarily defeating the effects of Dr. Fear's influence, and freeing the people who had been captured by his wrath, Captain Breakthrough took his usual three skip-steps forward and soared away.

As the wind whipped through his hair, Breakthrough realized that the forward progress he had made with the crowd through his motivational words would be short-lived. Dr. Fear was here to stay, and Breakthrough sensed it. Although many battles would ensue, he continued to focus solely on his goal - his end result to help the people overcome their fears - not concerning himself with how it would come to be.

The obstacle of fear was the subject I had chosen to speak on that night. As with every speech I had ever presented, in the moments before my name was introduced, I felt it again - the same fear that always seemed to grab me just before I took the platform. Everyone had always told me this was normal, so over time, I had learned how to use it to my advantage, and channel the energy into excitement as I addressed my audience.

Fear was also something I had become very familiar with from the various challenges I had dealt with over the years. As I sat running through the notes for my speech, I was suddenly catapulted back to when I first encountered Captain Breakthrough, my childhood idol.

I was just eight years old, and my dog Jack and I lived out every scene of "Captain Breakthrough," a popular Saturday morning TV show. My father, with his usual creative imagination, used my infatuation and fascination with this character to teach me many valuable life lessons.

I later realized that the lessons my father taught me were unique versions of the universal laws of success, which he brilliantly framed in a way that only the wildly imaginative mind of an eight-year-old could fully understand.

"Wow, Jack! Wasn't Captain Breakthrough awesome today? He's the COOLEST!" I said, rolling to my back on the floor of the family room. Now staring at the ceiling, dreaming about all the possibilities, I continued to wonder aloud, with Jack looking on in blank amazement.

"Just THINK about what he said, boy," I said magically to Jack.

"He makes me feel like I'm ten feet tall and can do ANYTHING. It's like I'm indestructible. I gotta' start thinking about only good stuff, just like he said, 'cause I want nothing more than to BE Captain Breakthrough. YOU'RE gonna be my sidekick as we fight Dr. Fear TOGETHER!" I continued on, with Jack by my side.

"All right Gordy," Dad called, "Turn the TV off; it's time to start your day."

I jumped up from the floor, and ran to the bathroom, although to me, it felt as if I was flying. As I began to brush my teeth, I wondered how Dad *knew* that my new favorite show had just finished. *Did he watch the show as well?* I wondered to myself. *Maybe he's got some kind of magical superpower that I don't know about*, my thoughts continued.

"OR MAYBE IT'S A PLOY!" I said aloud, as my thoughts quickly shifted.

"Maybe he's been contracted by Dr. Fear to suck the positivity from me, and they've assigned him this 'fatherly looking' body," my imagination expanded.

"I *think* Dad's one of us, Jack, but we can't be too careful," I confidently said to my white, fluffy dog, sure that he was clinging to every word, and taking mental notes.

When winter turned to spring, Jack and I would spend more time outside on Saturdays. This was where the real magic would start to happen. No more did I have to rely on inside props to accompany Captain Breakthrough on his missions, many of which I invented through my own imagination (although he willingly and gladly took part by breaking through every challenge right along with me).

I was the young protégé, the heir apparent to Breakthrough's title. I would one day too, inherent legions of adoring fans and followers. I would BE Captain Breakthrough, and save mankind from the horrible acts that Dr. Fear was sure to improve upon by the time I took over.

"I have to be prepared Jack - I must succeed!" I shouted, raising my hand-made PMA shield to the sky.

"This is my chance to work harder than anyone else to gain Captain Breakthrough's title. I want to become invincible. Like Captain Breakthrough, I will break through ANYTHING in my path. This will be my chief aim!" I went on as though I were on some sort of platform, like I had seen Dad do so many times.

One day, my imagination got the better of me, so Jack and I snuck quietly into the main linen closet. There, I strategically wrapped one of Mom's favorite flowered bed sheets around my neck. Then, with one of her dark lipsticks that she seldom used, which I assumed was for special occasions, I proudly drew a bold, red "B" right across the chest of the shirt I had selected for the day's adventure.

Jack looked at me with his head titled to one side.

Mom shook her head with a grin when I flew by her as she read one of her favorite magazines on the couch.

"Success is a mindset!" I shouted during my fly by, mimicking Captain Breakthrough. It wasn't until the third pass that Mom realized I had utilized one of her favorite bed sheets to represent my cape, until I was able to secure the flame retardant material I sought in my mind. Although she still smiled, I could tell that she was wondering what else I had gotten into to complete my uniform.

Dad told me once that I had inherited his personality and imagination. He always complemented me and told me that my grades were really good. He encouraged me to think and watch what I said. One of his famous sayings was, "Once you declare it, it's real." He had also taught me to look at any problem as merely a challenge - an opportunity to learn something new and to use my curious nature. So, by following his advice and using my curiosity, I remained positive and found the solution to many of my problems more easily.

"You spend a lot of time thinking about Captain Breakthrough, don't you, son? Why is that?" Dad asked in a tone that sounded like the question was leading to some kind of lesson.

"'Cause I want to BE him, Dad."

"Well, you know that what you think about most, you become, so you are on the right track there, son. Do you know what a 'chief aim' is?" Dad's questioning continued.

I shook my head, but I knew no matter what it was, it sounded good to me.

"It's a clear, specific goal for your entire life. For example, mine is to become one of the most sought-after motivational speakers in the world... so what would be your chief aim, Gordy?"

He had caught me off guard because I thought I had made it perfectly clear that I wanted to be a Superhero.

"Daaaaaad! I wanna be a Superhero like Captain Breakthrough!" I again pleaded my case.

"Ah yes, that's right. A Superhero. Now you *are* aware that becoming a Superhero is one of the hardest things in life to do, right son?" Dad asked.

"Hard?"

"Oooh yeah. Becoming a Superhero takes YEARS of practice, and during all that practice, you're going to fail a LOT. And the failure is a big part of what gives you the life experience needed to become a Superhero," Dad said, philosophically.

"How do you think Captain Breakthrough learns?"

I was stunned. I had a love-hate relationship with many of Dad's questions, because I knew they would somehow force me to think in order to come up with an intelligent answer – I just wanted to have fun.

"I guess I see what ya mean, Dad. But I'm up for the task! My chief aim is to BECOME Captain Breakthrough!" I said, confidently and proudly.

"Some people go through their entire lives never having an aim at all," Dad explained, "and they think that life is something that happens to them, and that they have no control over it. Like a ship on the water with no course. They just drift where the current takes them."

I listened intently, because I always seemed to get valuable nuggets of information from Dad.

"Now that you've figured out your chief aim, Gordy, you need to *really* focus on it…like a laser. Like when Captain Breakthrough decided to become a Superhero…he focused on it, and figured out the best way to achieve it," Dad went on.

"That's called a *burning desire*."

Dad explained, in simple terms, how important it was for me to always figure out what I wanted and focus on it with all my energy. Getting what I wanted all started from my thoughts, he said, and at that moment, I began to realize just how important my thoughts were.

"I have to go, Dad. The world NEEDS me! I have to STOP Dr. Fear!" I yelled, as I confidently tossed the sheet over my shoulder and soared out of the living room.

As I walked toward the platform of the huge convention hall where I had been hired as the guest speaker of the evening, I heard the emcee read through the introduction I had provided. It was almost time to go on stage.

I was giving a motivational address to a large group of entrepreneurs, and I knew that the words coming from my lips that evening would flow from my heart, as I reflected on all the lessons I learned so creatively from my dad.

Over the last several years, my dream of becoming a Superhero, and following in Dad's footsteps of being a sought-after motivational speaker, had become a reality. Waiting for the introduction to end so I could make my entrance onto the platform, I felt like Captain Breakthrough. After what seemed like an eternity, and with everyone on their feet in obvious anticipation of the message I was about to share, I could almost feel my cape behind me. As the applause came to a slow end, I cleared my throat, and you could hear a pin drop in the room.

I had the complete attention of every person in the room, and just like Captain Breakthrough would have done, I began my message of positivity.

As my speech came to a close, the applause thundered throughout the room. People rose to their feet and, as I stood savoring the moment, I thought about my dad. Facing one's fear was only one of many lessons he had taught me.

I took three skip-steps down from the platform and, before lurching into flight off the side of the stage, I turned and delivered my parting words for the night, which reminded me of the very first lesson I had learned from Captain Breakthrough:

"Success is a mindset!"

Chapter 1: Thinking Like A Superhero

I walked off the stage and, looking down, I grinned. Suddenly, I was back in time, not wearing my custom pin-striped suit, but my familiar blue cape.

BREAKTHROUGH SUCCESS TIP #1

Think hard about what you really want because what you think about most, becomes real!

"OUR THOUGHTS ARE TRAITORS AND MAKE US LOSE THE GOOD WE OFT MIGHT WIN BY FEARING TO ATTEMPT."

WILLIAM SHAKESPEARE

— Chapter 2 —
Constructing An Indestructible Cape

Chaos was starting to spread. Captain Breakthrough saw it everywhere. The local news, the Internet, and every other media outlet available were filled with news of Dr. Fear gaining strength.

"Drat! This menace is relentless. It's as if Fear never sleeps!" Breakthrough uttered, exasperated.

In his usual daily global sky observations, Breakthrough landed on yet another scene where it was reported Dr. Fear was wreaking havoc. Only this time, things were different, as there was a strange, distinct cloud of darkness present amongst the people. Captain Breakthrough had experienced the mental impact of fear many times during his life challenges. But never once had he experienced fear at such an amplified level. He could almost taste it.

Breakthrough turned from side to side, carefully scanning the area to see what was different. Then, off to the left, he noticed a large, dark, murky presence that he couldn't quite make out from behind the cloud. He knew this was something he had not seen before.

This has to be the infamous Dr. Fear, he said quietly to himself.

The hunchbacked man, cloaked in black, clenched his hands in fists of rage.

"Life is a HOPELESS endeavor. All you can do is limp through existence, just trying to survive," he said in a piercingly evil tone. He was unaware Breakthrough was on the scene.

Dr. Fear continued his negative siege and let out a hair-raising cackle directed to all who were present, pausing after each sentence of his negative rhetoric.

Captain Breakthrough could not believe his ears. Dr. Fear was saying everything he could to cause people to doubt themselves. He was instructing them to worry about needless things. He encouraged them to stress out over negative events that hadn't even happened yet. He wanted them to have no self-esteem and to hate their lives and their jobs...and most horribly, to feel hopeless about their futures. Captain Breakthrough realized that Dr. Fear had embraced fear in astronomic proportions, and was using its energy to fuel his own diabolical motives. Dr. Fear was powerful and the most frightening thing about him was he knew it!

Dr. Fear displayed sinister self-confidence as he continued on his tyrannical speech.

"My Robotic Thought Vacuum will allow me to take control of the world. As I suck the life out of every willing victim, I'm loving every minute of it!" he said urgently, and with growing ferocity as he waved the remote control for his machine into the air.

Breakthrough, careful yet confident, begin to take large strides toward Dr. Fear. Upon noticing the man donned with a blue cape flapping in the wind behind him, Dr. Fear stopped his dialogue, interested in this man. His eyes were barely visible beneath his hooded black cloak, and his bushy eyebrows bristled just enough to convey a sense of evil. Dr. Fear glared at the confident young man and took note of the shield upon his arm.

As Breakthrough quickly approached the imposing, dark figure, he held up his left hand and pointed at Dr. Fear while his right arm confidently displayed his PMA Shield.

"You think you are very powerful, Dr. Fear," Captain Breakthrough yelled, "but you'll never be powerful enough to stop the super power of belief, confident decisions, positive autosuggestion, and most importantly - self-confidence!" he retorted.

Seeing the emblazoned B on the bulging chest of the caped man, Dr. Fear sensed who it was. Though they had never met, Dr. Fear was keenly aware of any source of resistance to his wicked plan. In the past, many had tried to thwart his spread of negativity, but none had been a true challenge. He had been waiting for a nemesis to appear. He knew that for every negative force, a positive counterpart exists.

"Fiiiiiinally, Captain Breakthrough...we meet at last," he said, baring his rotting, crooked teeth.

"Be warned; any attempt to stop me is hopeless. I am much too powerful for you," he growled, pointing at Breakthrough with his knotted knuckles.

"The people...all around the world...are starting to follow meeeee, and you will not be able to stop the powerful shroud of negativity I'm veiling over every mind on the planet," he went on, as he continued to chuckle confidently.

"I will soon CONTROL THE WORLD!" his shrill voice rang out in discord.

Breakthrough stood there and endured the gruesome character's dialogue before he replied quickly, and abruptly.

"Your induced fear is temporary, Doctor...positivity WILL prevail. I'll make sure of it. You will NOT win!" Breakthrough said, as he looked squarely into the face of Fear.

Dr. Fear, unaffected by Breakthrough's words, replied.

"What you don't seem to understand, is that I hold the keys to every human's mind in the world. Once I control their mental cores, ALL belief in themselves will disappear, and they will become subservient to me forever!" Dr. Fear responded in an evil, but steady voice.

Captain Breakthrough knew that if Fear were to succeed in this diabolical scheme, that the future of mankind would be bleak, at best. Without the ability to think decisively, act positively, and choose wisely with a clear mind, human beings would begin a fast downward spiral into powerlessness. Once they lost their belief in themselves, their self-confidence would surely depart soon after. He knew he had only moments to make a life-altering decision about what to do . . .

Captain Breakthrough turned his back on Fear, and began to speak firmly, and with the utmost of confidence, to the people who had gathered. He began to explain a very important subject unknown to the masses.

"Your subconscious mind IS the superpower within, and until you learn how to use both the conscious mind, and subconscious mind, for their respective purposes, success will elude you and you will be vulnerable to the grip of fear. Reprogram your mind by telling yourself only

positive things," he exclaimed to the entire area.

"Your subconscious mind is nothing more than a high-powered computer that must be instructed about what you want and how to think. Then, and ONLY then, can it instruct your conscious mind how to respond to outside stimulus in your daily life," his speech continued.

"So, by speaking positive affirmations about your goals and desires aloud every day, you are programming your mind toward the success you desire," he continued.

His eyes began to focus on the people who had gathered around. It was vital that they listened to every word, or fear would take over. As he ended his speech, Captain Breakthrough quickly realized that he was going to have to keep an eye on fear at all times, for it can be sneaky and elusive. Dr. Fear had disappeared, unfazed by Captain Breakthrough's inspirational speech. Although he had faded from view, Breakthrough sensed Dr. Fear was still on the scene.

"Dr. Fear, you will not succeed, because people are learning the power of autosuggestion," Captain Breakthrough began to announce in all directions. With his PMA shield proudly displayed on his right arm, he continued.

"Winning and succeeding at the highest level is only a positive attitude away, and the people will soon realize that" he went on, but spoke louder now, so everyone could hear.

"Happiness comes from freedom, and freedom comes from doing what you want to do...this starts with belief in yourself, belief in your ideas, and thinking bigger than big!" he bellowed.

Dr. Fear then stepped out from the shadows and stared at Captain Breakthrough. Although it appeared he was listening to every word, Dr. Fear's mind was fixated on his own agenda: becoming the most dominant, fear-inspiring entity anyone had ever experienced, and controlling the world. This was a perfect example of using the power of programming the subconscious mind.

"RUBBISH!" Fear screamed.

"It's all rubbish…no one believes in their dreams anymore…take a look around you, Breakthrough. Only a select few people ever win big in life. By getting everyone to realize this, I will mold the minds of ALL mankind forever," Dr. Fear screamed. He turned away, disgusted, and quickly disappeared again into the same shroud of darkness from which he had just appeared.

Captain Breakthrough knew defeating Dr. Fear was going to be more difficult than he imagined. He knew that Fear's negative outlook was just what the masses typically clung to, and, if allowed to get too far out of control, would be difficult to overcome.

With the people now restored to a more positive mindset, and Dr. Fear nowhere around, Captain Breakthrough spoke quietly with local authorities about the gravity of the situation. He gave them instructions on what needed to be stated to the media, so the public would only hear affirmations of positivity. As he turned to leave, he spoke aloud.

"Don't worry. I'm here to help defeat Dr. Fear, but it's going to take effort from everyone. I'm still in the preliminary stage of development, but I'm working on a contraption that will aid our efforts," he confided.

He turned, grabbed his cape, which was now flowing over the front of his right shoulder, and tossed it back. He took three skip-steps forward, and before anyone realized, Captain Breakthrough was in flight. Now, although his mind was racing, he had total belief and self-confidence that he would conquer Dr. Fear.

He flew through the clouds; his face collecting moisture as he entered and departed each one. He began to reflect back on his Superhero training. The familiar positive affirmations for overcoming fear, continuing to take steps toward mastering his craft, and achieving his life's purpose, began to go through his mind quietly.

He swiftly flew on as the sky suddenly turned a solid blue, with no more clouds in sight. Soaring high above the ground, the mental affirmations running through his mind triggered his voice to speak them aloud.

"I am powerful, and I can do this…I will defeat Dr. Fear and anything his evil mind can concoct." He spoke loud enough so he could hear his words through the roaring wind. He stated it over and over again, and as he did, his confidence grew even more.

"I AM Captain Breakthrough, and I can do anything I set my mind to do!" The affirmations grew larger.

"No one and NOTHING will stand in my way. I am a Superhero!" The power of auto-suggestion was now strengthening his subconscious mind, and Breakthrough knew it.

On my drive home from the convention center where I had just given one of my best speeches to date, I was completely lost in thought. As I drove, I pondered not only my performance and how I could improve for next time, but also the impact both Captain Breakthrough, and my dad, had had on my life.

I reached down to turn on the radio, thinking some light classical music would enhance my thoughts. In the blink of an eye, I looked up and saw a 12-point buck standing in the road just ahead. He was motionless, and staring at me like it was a showdown. I knew I had to make a fast decision.

In a matter of seconds, I felt my body turn stiff as I slammed on the brakes. My white knuckles gripped the steering wheel and jerked it to one side in an effort to avoid the deer. I came to a screeching halt on the side of the road, as I watched the deer gallop off into the black night from my rear view mirror. I gathered myself, and let my heart rate slow down a bit before continuing my trek home. Again, I reached down to turn on the radio, hoping the classical music would soothe my mind.

As I reveled in the soft sounds, I began to think

how – in the blink of an eye – my thoughts had quickly turned to fear when the deer appeared. It was almost as though the intense positive feelings I had been having were sucked from every orifice in my body.

I began to chuckle a bit, as I remembered how impressed I was with Dr. Fear's Robotic Thought Vacuum. My chuckle turned to outright laughter as I realized just how outlandish this whole contraption was, but at the same time, what a great analogy it turned out to be for my dad. As he always did, he managed to turn this outrageous device into a great life lesson for me.

At the time, I was so caught up in the story that the producers of Captain Breakthrough provided every week in the TV show, that I was completely oblivious to their underlying lessons. Thankfully, Dad was savvy enough to realize just how brilliant the producers of the show were, and decided to take the valuable lessons and teach me, at a young age, the universal laws of success I carry with me to this day.

"If I'm going to defeat Dr. Fear, I need more muscle. I wonder what's the quickest way to get beefed up?" I asked, as I stared my dog squarely into his eyes.

"THAT'S IT! I have it, I know what to do…" and I galloped off to enact my plan.

I immediately soared to Dad and Mom's bedroom in search of something to beef up my small, but growing body, and began my strategic ransacking.

"I have to protect the world from Dr. Fear, so Mom will understand…won't she, Jack?" I thought hesitantly as I thrust myself onto their bed and proceeded to dismember their down pillows.

I could feel myself getting stronger just as quickly as I could stuff the smooth, silky down into my shirt. Although Jack thought it was playtime and was frolicking in the mess I was making, he quickly snapped to attention as I soared back into flight and made an announcement.

"Let's go boy! Now we can go get that Dr. Fear!"

With a trail of white feathers behind me, and my loyal, white fluffy sidekick by my side, I was confident that Dr. Fear was doomed.

"Now all I have to do is figure out how to thwart the Robotic Thought Vacuum," I said to Jack.

As the day went on, I was consumed with thoughts of soaring through the air fighting fear and negativity around the world. I was covertly leaning against a tree in the backyard, and starting to tremble a bit, as I began to wonder about how Mom would react to my strategic use of her pillows. All of a sudden, I heard the blood-curdling rendition of my name that I knew was only capable from Mom's lungs.

"GOOOOOORDY!" she screamed.

Something told me Mom didn't see the same importance in using her down pillows to pad my muscles as I did. I bravely absorbed the verdict of my sentence from Mom, while Dad stood in the background. I took my punishment like a Superhero and figured I could use the confinement to my room as valuable time for me to plan my next attack on Dr. Fear.

Later that day, about an hour into my sentence, Dad came into my room. I was hopeful that he would somehow be able to negotiate my early release, but I quickly realized that my parole date had been set and was non-negotiable.

"I understand your need for strength, son, but how do you feel about the decision you made to use Mom's pillows?" Dad asked.

Before I had a chance to utter a word, he continued in a stern, but encouraging voice.

"You've got to use your creative mind to be MUCH more strategic with your decisions, son. The way I see it, I'm not so sure you thought the pillow thing all the way through," Dad said.

I didn't want to hear it, but I knew he was right, as usual.

"I know I made a mistake, Dad, but I've GOT to get back out there...the world NEEDS me!" I pleaded.

"Fighting fear is a mental battle, not a physical one, son. Yes, you DO have to face fear head-on, but it all starts in the mind, just like Captain Breakthrough said," Dad continued.

All I could do was bow my head, and as Jack rested his chin on my leg, I continued to listen to what Dad had to say.

"Gordy, there lies within each of us a sleeping power. It's actually a 'super' power, just like Captain Breakthrough has. And once you learn how to harness this power, you can create *any* outcome in life you desire. However, if this power is left to run wild, you can cause yourself great distress and needless suffering. That is why having a passionate, chosen course for your life is crucial."

As Dad instilled more of his life philosophy in me, a smirk came across his lips. Suddenly, his eyes shifted to one side, then the other.

"What was THAT?!" he said, shocked.

Alarmed, I too looked side to side. As Jack stood perked at full attention, wondering what the heck was going on, Dad continued.

"I think I just heard Dr. Fear…he may be lurking outside…" he went on in a confident, yet somewhat scary, tone of voice.

"This is something only YOU can handle, son…I trust you. You have your mind, and it's more powerful than even Dr. Fear, so use it wisely and protect us from harm! I'll protect Mom, but I'm counting on you to protect everyone else. Put that powerful mind of yours to work…just keep saying 'I can do this, I can do this, I can do this'…Captain Breakthrough will be waiting for you after you've served your time," he said, almost in a whisper. His eye offered a subtle wink in my direction as he left the room.

Now convinced that Dad was the real deal, and not under the influence of Dr. Fear, I pulled out the journal Dad had given me for my birthday two months earlier and began to sketch out my ideas. My confidence was high.

The two weeks that I was sentenced to solitary confinement in my bedroom dragged by, and I couldn't mark the X's off on my wall calendar fast enough. After what seemed like an eternity, my time was about up. My sentence was almost complete. I now knew that down pillows made for horrible muscles and, more importantly, a hasty, bad decision. I needed to strengthen my mind.

The Saturday after my grounding, as another episode of Captain Breakthrough came to a close, I couldn't help but wonder, *He has his PMA shield, but will it take MORE to defeat Dr. Fear and his evil machine once and for all?*

Mom interrupted my thought to say breakfast was ready.

As I looked up, pride burst from her face, and I could tell she knew that my sentence had ensured that her bedroom was now safe.

"Dad, Dr. Fear's Robotic Thought Vacuum must be stopped! I have to help Captain Breakthrough with his contraption to combat it, before we all are rendered LIFELESS!" I proclaimed as I lurched emphatically into the kitchen.

"Gordy, the subconscious adoption of an idea originates in thought, but it becomes real through repetition of verbal statements. Remember when we discussed this? This is why you hear Captain Breakthrough saying positive affirmations so often," Dad said.

"Dr. Fear is powerful because he uses his subconscious mind for evil, and he's let himself become controlled by fearful thoughts. His Robotic Thought Vacuum is an extreme representation of just how powerful fear can be in stealing positive thoughts," Dad continued.

"But Dad, I *know* I can save the world from Dr. Fear's tyranny of negative thoughts, and the only way I can do that is to become a Superhero like Captain Breakthrough!" I argued.

Yet again, Dad wryly questioned me, as I reinforced to him that I was going to become a Superhero when I grew up.

"Are you *really* sure you two are up for the task?" he asked motioning to me and Jack.

"Up to the task? Dad, we've talked about this," I replied almost indignantly.

"This is all Jack and I ever talk about...fighting off all the wrong that Dr. Fear throws at the world. It's my destiny, I just BELIEVE IT!" A sound of strong self-confidence expelled as my chest inflated. I sternly angled my chin upward, threw Mom's sheet back over my right shoulder, and let my dad know that I was not fazed by such a remark.

"Well, all I mean, Son, is that it's not easy being a Superhero. I know we've talked about this a little before, but there's a lot of responsibility and preparatory work that must go into it. Remember, *with great power, comes great responsibility.* More responsibility than what they talk about during the show. I fully believe in you, and will always encourage you to do anything you want to do, but it's very important that you know the challenges you're going to face if you pursue the life of a Superhero," Dad said in his usual, supportive way.

"What da' ya' mean, Dad?" I asked in a tone that clearly indicated I knew what I was doing, but wanted to make him feel good by engaging in dialogue.

"Well, the work you're putting in now is great," he said, "and also very admirable, but this is only the beginning," he continued. I sat down and started to show more interest.

I wonder what more could be involved, I thought. I was determined to figure out what inside information Dad had. I was certain it would give me an edge.

I continued to listen intently to what Dad had to say about everything that I needed to learn to become a real Superhero.

"On TV you see all the *benefits* of being a Superhero, and that looks exciting right? You know…the flying through the air…the saving people…the cool contraptions…"

"Right, and the *super* adventures," I added.

"But, they don't discuss *all* the little steps you need to take to get there," Dad continued.

"Being a real Superhero involves far more than just being strong physically and saving people from Dr. Fear and the strife that most people experience. It's also about *mastering* the laws of Superhero Success®."

"What are the laws?" I asked honestly.

"This is something that cannot be answered quickly, Gordy," Dad said instructively.

"This is something that takes even the smartest, most determined person a long time, sometimes even years to learn, through experience, education, mentorship, coaching, and thought, like I mentioned before. And this is why only about three out of every hundred people that set out to achieve success, or become a Superhero, ever make it."

"You make it sound difficult."

"There's a reason why this is true. If success were easy, son, everyone would experience it. Those who do achieve success live a fulfilling life. If you want to become a Superhero, I'll be behind you every step of the way, because I want you to live the exact life you choose for yourself, and nothing less. If you're up for the challenge, then I will help you become a Superhero, and when you get older, you can have and do everything you want. You already display many of the qualities of a Superhero, and that's why I feel you are ready to learn all I am teaching you."

"Hey you two, your breakfast is getting cold," Mom exclaimed just as Dad's words began to make me feel like I was walking on air."

"Let's focus on refueling, Gordy. Your mom took the time to make breakfast for us, so let's show our appreciation by telling her how thankful we are that she made it for us, OK?" Dad suggested.

"Then afterwards, we'll continue our discussion. Deal?"

I really didn't have to think too hard.

"It's a deal!" I said with agreement as I dug into my pancakes. I was completely lost in thought, so excited, and somehow mesmerized, by everything Dad just told me.

I finally arrived home safely after my encounter with the deer. As I pulled into the driveway, a sense of peace came over me, and I immediately thought of my wife and kids, who awaited me inside. As I stepped inside my home, I reflected on how I had learned the laws of success, and how being a Superhero was indeed a lifelong pursuit, as Dad had suggested to me so many years before. I glanced around and, as Dad had predicted, I had been able to design the life I wanted. But, as I proudly looked at my home, I realized that I would never really be done; as long as I had my mind, there would always be mental work to do.

BREAKTHROUGH SUCCESS TIP #2

Control your mind, not the other way around!

"A GOAL IS A DREAM WITH A DEADLINE."

- DR. NAPOLEON HILL

— Chapter 3 —
Developing X-ray Vision

Captain Breakthrough finally made it back to his secluded lair in the mountains. It was the one place he could let his imagination expand, and concentrate fully. He had hopes of getting some much-needed rest, but his mind was still racing.

Dr. Fear was gaining strength at an alarming rate. Captain Breakthrough needed to complete a machine to help him in this battle, and it was going to require more than just accurate thinking. It was going to require *vision*.

"It's my imagination that allows me to look beyond the current circumstances," he uttered to himself.

"...And it's my imagination that provides my VISION..." his voice began to raise.

"And THIS is my x-ray vision!" he commanded to the empty room around him.

"And my x-ray vision will help me find a solution to this vexing conundrum!" his voice rang out in confirmation.

He quickly reflected back to one of his favorite courses at the Academy - one in which he had learned the subtle nuances of x-ray vision. The most beneficial use of this talent is the ability to see through obstacles and challenges in order to focus on the solution. He would need to utilize this tool in his arsenal against Fear, for motivational speeches and the PMA shield would only go so far in his efforts to help the people.

Hoping for the best, but preparing for the worst, Breakthrough believed a good night's rest would clear his mind and bring answers to some of the questions that still taunted him. He went to bed late, still deep in thought over the perplexing situation.

Early the next morning, Breakthrough was woken abruptly by the incessant beeping alarm of his negativity sensing computer software. The screen was lit up like a Christmas tree, showing the "hot spots" of negative activity. Notifications had been pouring in all night from around the world, each one summoning him for help. Breakthrough acted decisively and quickly took action.

Immediately, he gathered his thoughts and reached toward the ceiling as he stretched his arms and body from the short night's sleep. He yawned and shook his head abruptly, dragging his large, rugged fingers through his thick, dark hair. With a sigh, Captain Breakthrough pondered, *Every time I battle Fear, he seems to get stronger...*

"Maybe I'm spending too much energy focusing on the problem and not enough time focusing on the solution," he curiously said aloud.

He quickly assembled his dashing uniform, completing the ensemble by attaching the thick, silk cape around his neck. Then, Captain Breakthrough was quickly speeding through the air to tend to the wrath that Dr. Fear had inflicted on the unknowing people.

One by one, Breakthrough raced to each "hot spot" of negativity. He descended into the heart of every scene of turmoil...one leg straight with foot pointed down, the other leg slightly bent, he seemed to come out of nowhere, softly gliding to a secure landing in each different location. His blue cape was a vision of dominance as it flapped in the wind.

Each time, he would use his power of positivity and give his usual motivational speech of encouragement, stressing the importance of owning and controlling your thoughts.

"Concentrate solely on what you WANT," he would say demandingly, "not on what you don't want. Do you want your entire lives to be ruled by Fear," he asked rhetorically, "or do you want to live a lifestyle of your own design?" he further questioned, this time as though he wanted them to scream the obvious answer aloud.

"If you're thinking and believing what someone else is telling you, then you are not thinking accurately" Breakthrough continued.

He could sense people were listening to him with a knowingness that he was right, but he could see Dr. Fear already had a strangle hold on every mind. It was at that moment he realized how Fear was able to take over different areas simultaneously.

"He must have RELEASED the Robotic Thought Vacuum *nationally!*" Captain Breakthrough said, clenching his fist and gritting his teeth.

Dr. Fear *had* expanded the reach of The Robotic Thought Vacuum, his powerful weapon of mass mental destruction. In numerous cities around the nation, the vengeful focus of Dr. Fear had intensified. He fixated on the mental anguish he intended to broadcast to the people, as a way to control their minds.

Earlier, Breakthrough had seen only a fraction of the damage that the Robotic Thought Vacuum was capable of inflicting. He then realized in his earlier encounter with Dr. Fear that his nemesis was still in the testing phase of his device. As the kinks in his diabolical machine had been ironed out, the Robotic Thought Vacuum had increased its negative influence. It had started to affect more and more people. Even worse, there was evidence that some of Dr. Fear's victims were beginning to band together in a cultish movement. Fear had unknowingly started developing fear disciples..."Fear Mongers."

The media was following the wrath of Dr. Fear, and during their investigation it was revealed that he had been constructing his Robotic Thought Vacuum for the past several years. It was an elaborate satellite that was entirely powered by negativity. Strategically, he had positioned it in outer space for the purposes of telepathically sucking positive thoughts from vulnerable minds while simultaneously sending out mental seeds of vacuous fearful thoughts. The device was clearly aimed at all those who didn't have goals, those who didn't have desires, and people with no chief aim for their lives. These waves of vacuous thoughts then quickly lead to confusion, inaction, and literal paralysis.

When Captain Breakthrough descended on the last of the cities affected by Dr. Fear's current tour of destruction, he once again came face to face with his nemesis, easily spotting Fear's horrendous haze of darkness.

Although Breakthrough quickly took out his PMA shield to battle

Dr. Fear, the waves of negativity slowly began to overtake him. Captain Breakthrough held the shield in front of him, locked in concentration.

"I will destroy you and your Robotic Thought Vacuum," he said, as he directed his statement toward Dr. Fear.

"I've imagined your demise over and over again in my mind. I've sworn to protect the people of this planet, and YOU will be eliminated," he said assertively, yet calmly, toward Dr. Fear.

"I have my PMA shield, and it protects me from all your negativity. I will use my mind to figure out a way to destroy your machine and offer power to the people by teaching them to harness their thoughts and placing them within their own mental shield."

"Put that thing away!" Dr. Fear said, diabolically.

"You'll need more than a shield, Breakthrough! I can take ANY man's thoughts and break him down into a sniveling, pathetic, wandering zombie. All your PMA paraphernalia will do you no good, and will do NO ONE any good," Dr. Fear hissed, franticly.

"The people are slowly learning the secrets of success, and they know how to distinguish between your lies and their own accurate thinking," Captain Breakthrough said, as he swooped down and stuck his PMA shield right in Dr. Fear's face.

"Ha! The masses think that's WAY too much work," Dr. Fear began.

"By the time I'm done with them they will fear EVERYTHING! They will be pathetic victims of their own perceived circumstance, paralyzed into inaction where they will be mine FOREVER!" Fear thundered.

"My Robotic Thought Vacuum will allow me to suck any sign of a positive thought right out of them!" Dr. Fear chuckled in a nefarious, sadistic way, as he scurried out of sight.

As always, Breakthrough did what he could to restore positivity to the area, and instructed the people on the power of their own minds. However, he soon realized that the effects of Dr. Fear and The Robotic Thought Vacuum were becoming more ingrained in people's minds.

Before he had departed each of the affected areas, Captain Breakthrough had spent time interviewing witnesses. He uncovered startling pieces of information common amongst the scenes. Although Breakthrough had encountered Dr. Fear on the scene in only one location, witnesses reported that they definitely felt Fear's presence in each of the areas. Captain Breakthrough learned that people saw different shadowy entities at each scene, but that none of the figures actually fit the description of Dr. Fear himself. Each city seemed to be dominated by a different, yet very specific, negative influence. *Does fear change its appearance? Does it rear its ugly head in different forms?* Captain Breakthrough wondered. He was perplexed, but determined to find an answer to his questions. *What is Dr. Fear up to?* his thoughts continued.

Knowing he still had work to do, and that the people were safe for now, Captain Breakthrough prepared to leave the last scene. He knew he needed to stretch his imagination and focus on the most viable solution to this perplexing challenge.

Breakthrough concentrated his mental efforts back in the safety of his secret lair. He began to compile any information he could about fear and contemplate what could be the underlying motivation of Dr. Fear's vindictive and vengeful scheme. He knew that if he could uncover the root cause of Dr. Fear's suffering, he'd be better able to quickly disarm this heavily burdened man.

I am sure that a positive mental attitude will beat this guy, Breakthrough thought to himself.

"But I've GOT figure out a way to instill my positive mental attitude into my contraption, so it can have the exact opposite effect of Fear's Robotic Thought Vacuum," he said aloud.

As he paced furiously through his office, pondering what kind of impact his newly devised machine would have, he considered all the possibilities of how to annihilate Fear once and for all. His mind began to drift.

"What am I supposed to learn from all this?" Breakthrough wondered aloud.

As he continued to pace back and forth, concentrating on finding a

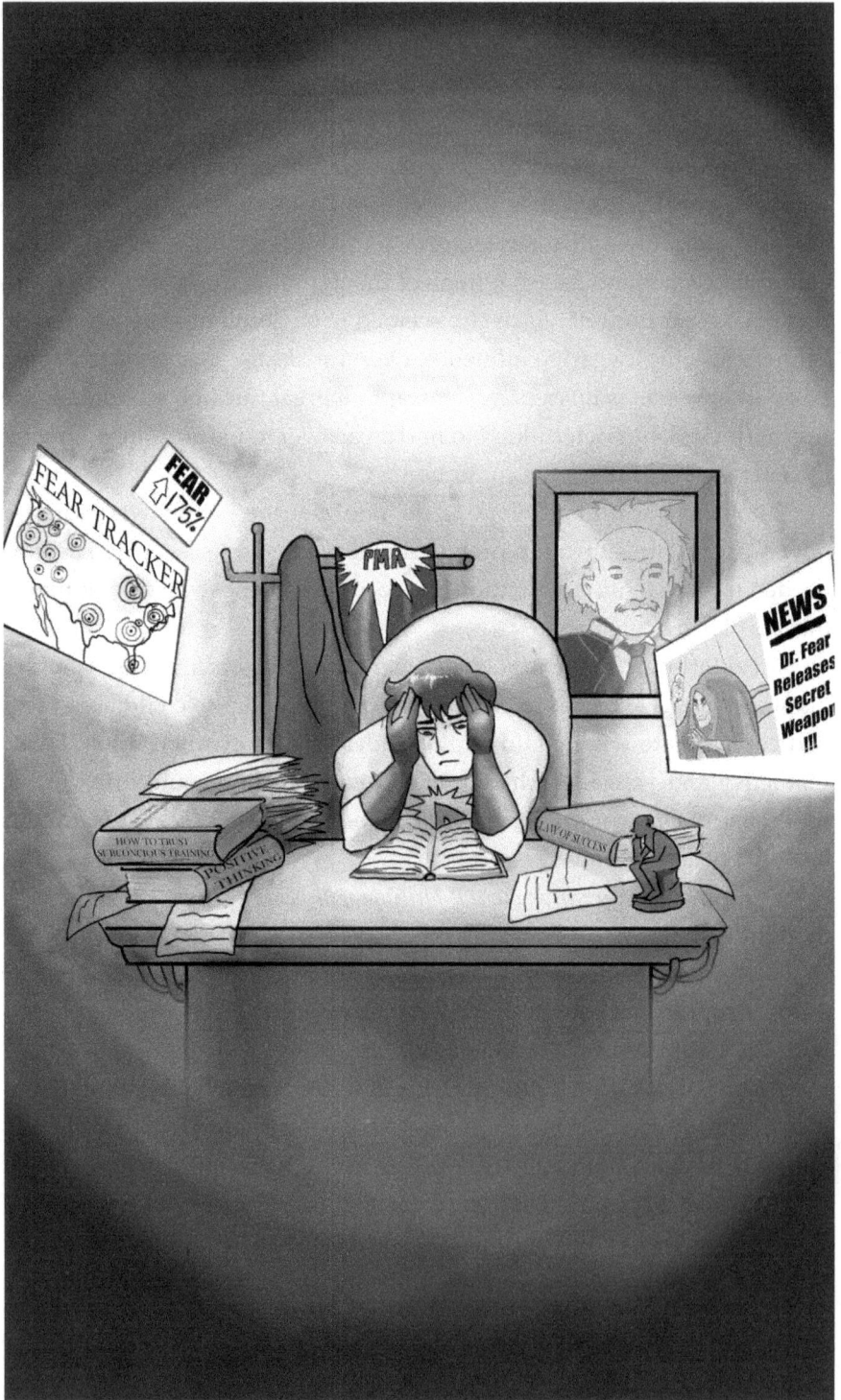

solution to this potentially disastrous conundrum, he noticed something strange began to happen. Clarity was beginning to form in his head. The concentration was working.

He began to journal his thoughts while they were fresh in his mind. He wrote furiously, one thought quickly leading to the next, as new ideas flooded his conscious brain. He couldn't write fast enough. Two hours passed quickly. Then he stopped, laughed out loud, then harder, and before he knew it, he was hunched down in his chair laughing hysterically, almost uncontrollably. The solution he had been seeking was right there in front of him! During this "brain dump," he had scribbled down everything he could uncover from the deep crevasses of his mind, and lo and behold, the missing component of the device he was developing had been realized.

Almost as though it had materialized from thin air, the solution appeared. Captain Breakthrough knew it was his own subconscious at work. During weeks of sleepless nights pondering this solution, the seed had been planted, and he knew that his subconscious mind continued to work on the problem, in the rare moments when he managed to get some rest. Breakthrough knew the magic of the human mind, but was still fascinated when the evidence of it appeared in his life like a super power.

I had locked myself in my office one night to concentrate on a new speech I wanted to develop, which involved the concept of fear, and its correlation to achieving success. After a rough day of dealing with printing and other fulfillment issues for my new home study program, my mind was searching for inspiration.

I surrounded myself with a select group of books from the vast library I had accumulated over the years. I began to sift through the pile of books, along with various magazines, highlighted articles, and hand written notes I had gathered. In the past, I had learned that the mind was an incredible instrument, and that inspiration sometimes appears out of nowhere, at the strangest of times. I knew that as I asked myself to find the inspirational nugget I was looking for, my subconscious was doing as I commanded.

Many thoughts and ideas crossed my mind as I continued to sift through the mass of information. It wasn't until I moved some loose papers from atop a stack of magazines that the inspiration I needed came to me in a very unsuspected way. An issue of National Geographic was glaring at me. The title read, "African Serengeti," and the cover showed a breathtaking photo of a herd of wildebeests in the setting sun. Immediately, I was transported back to the many frequent trips Dad and I took to the zoo when I was a kid. Since I was an only child, Dad always took a particular interest in one-on-one time with me, and the zoo was a place where we always bonded.

Thinking about those memories reminded me of the time I had my first fifteen minutes of fame and taste of success. I was a fearless eight-year-old...

"The problem with Ms. Shanahan is she teaches stuff that's not important!" I said as I paced back and forth across my bedroom, ranting about my teacher.

With Jack laying on the edge of my bed, his eyes drifting off into sleep, I continued my tirade.

"All she does is focus on the problem, not the SOLUTION! What possible good can I offer the world by learning about *fractions*? We don't see Captain *Breakthrough* wasting his time on studying fractions, do we Jack?"

Jack was clearly uninterested in my frustration, but I knew deep down that he wanted to annihilate Dr. Fear with me.

"We *need* to be studying the rules of *engagement*...and...and...how to construct genuine flame retardant capes...and...*important* stuff like *that!*" I continued to plead my case with Jack.

Now feeling hungry, I stopped pacing and looked up.

"Ya know, Jack…I'm with Captain Breakthrough! I'm kinda tired of battlin' Dr. Fear, too. I think it's time we regroup and reconvene tomorrow on the matter, after school," I told him, as I turned to go to the kitchen for a snack.

The next day at school, I was counting down the hours until the bell rang and I could fly home. I was ready to dawn my cape and shield, fight Dr. Fear, and start implementing these 'laws of success' Dad had mentioned the other day.

"I wonder what law he's going to teach me next? I bet it's going to be the law of DOMINATION and CONTROL!", I said under my breath in class. My thoughts began to wander in excitement.

Just as I was starting to become immersed in thoughts of crushing Dr. Fear with my knowledge of the laws Dad was teaching me, Ms. Shanahan dropped the bomb. It was the assignment of all assignments. Everyone had to write a story about their hero. My dad immediately jumped to my mind. The story was due the next day.

Knowing this assignment was going to severely hamper the available time I had already allotted to scan the global landscape and fight the crimes of negativity, I began to think about what story I could write. I knew I needed to think of something fast, so I could get the story written and be done with it. The world needed me for far more important matters.

Once home, I went straight to Dad to see if he could help me find inspiration for this "story," and also to rant about my dismay of having to deal with fractions.

"First things first, Gordy. Math is just as important as every other subject in school. You don't think Captain Breakthrough became the Superhero he is today by only learning about one or two subjects, do you?" Dad asked me, with a puzzled look on his face.

"Have you considered the knowledge of math he needs to be able to engineer all of his machines?" he added, emphatically.

I must have had a puzzled look on my face, because Dad looked at me with a little smile, and continued on, without giving me a chance to answer his apparently rhetorical question.

"Captain Breakthrough learned the skill of being a Superhero at the Academy by taking many different courses, but he also learned the art of Superhero Success™ through many long hours of study. And the time you spend studying all these different things, while you're still developing your Superhero skills, is when you determine which strengths you have and where your passions lie. Once you know what your strengths and passions are, you can decide where to focus your energies and develop specialized knowledge in one or more areas...does this make sense, Son?" he asked, now in a serious tone.

"I think so, Dad...so basically, I need to look at math as a stepping stone on my path to crush Dr. Fear and his wicked Robotic Thought Vacuum!" I stated, with only a slight question behind it.

"Exactly! You've got to stay positively focused, even when you have to do some things you may not like...this is your vision, son...err, your X-ray vision... your ability to see beyond the problem. Later on, your X-ray vision will be so strong you'll be able to see right through ANY problem!" Dad said.

"So once you know your path in life, you're much more able to focus on the solution to any challenge, instead of the problem," he assured.

As I was digesting everything Dad had just told me, I sat down in his cushy leather chair, which seemed to engulf me.

"So you have to write a story about your hero huh?" Dad stated, in a pondering tone of voice.

"What do you think Captain Breakthrough would do if faced with the same dilemma?" he asked.

"He'd use his imagination!" I quickly, and confidently, responded.

"Absolutely!" Dad retorted, as he put his hand on my head and messed up my hair.

"Um, can you give me a few ideas to get me started, Dad? I want to write about you." I asked, anxious to get back to dealing with Dr. Fear.

"Oh...I thought you would write about Captain Breakthrough," Dad said, in a surprised tone.

"Why would I write about him, he's got an ENTIRE show written about him! Dad, he's EVEN got a secret lair! My story is your chance to go BIG time, Dad...

just like Captain Breakthrough!" I exclaimed, excitedly.

"Oh wow...you're right," he said, with a secretive undertone.

"Good thinking, Son. OK...how about when you and I went to zoo a couple of months ago? Remember when you were disappointed after you found out your favorite animal, Nigel the gnu, had passed away? You were pretty affected by that, until we talked about the thoughts you were having."

I remembered how sad I was when I first heard Nigel had died. Dad talked to me about my thoughts, and helped me to remember the good feelings I had when I had sat for hours watching him play on the rocks. He helped me to examine my thoughts, and the feelings these thoughts generated. I realized it was easy to let thoughts turn negative based on something that happened. With Dad's help, I was quickly back on track, and delighted when the zoo soon adopted Neiko, a baby gnu.

"That's IT, Dad! I'll write about *that* time together!" I proclaimed.

Dad always said I needed to use my imagination, just like Captain Breakthrough did.

"What can I call the story?" I thought. After careful deliberation, "The New Gnu" was born.

Knowing that I needed supercharged nourishment for this highly mental exercise, I gave Dad a big hug and headed for the kitchen.

I downed my Superhero, high octane, super energy concoction of two bananas, doused with peanut butter and a handful of chocolate chips with each bite. Then I ran swiftly to my bedroom and proceeded to write my story.

Writing every detail of my experience to the best of my ability, and letting my imagination run freely, within one hour, my masterpiece was complete. I had to show Dad.

"This is an excellent display of your creative imagination, Son!" Dad said, as I proudly showed off my work.

"Captain Breakthrough would be proud! You displayed imagination, clear vision, deep concentration, and accurate thought. You know...I think you may very well get a scholarship to the Superhero Academy, just like Captain Breakthrough did" he went on, encouragingly.

Excited and confident that Dad was well on his way to obtaining his own secret lair with my story, I was once again in flight to figure out a way to defeat Fear's growing consortium.

Several days passed, and I continued to reflect on Dad's latest lessons while I plotted out Dr. Fear's demise. I was certain all I needed to do was spread my positivity to the world. One night, while I lay on the living room floor, battling with my Captain Breakthrough and Dr. Fear figurines, the phone rang.

"Oh, hi Ms. Shanahan!" Dad said to my teacher.

"What have I done?!" I whispered aloud to Jack who was lying next to me. My thoughts raced as I watched Dad nodding his head while uttering, "I understand…" to my teacher. I was sure I was doomed. Fearful thoughts immediately consumed my mind, as I wondered what I could have possibly done and forgotten about. As Dad handed the phone to Mom, my mind was reeling, trying to retrace my footsteps of the day. The only thing that stood out was that I had turned in the story I had written about the gnu.

"Well, young man…" Dad said in a reprimanding, but fun sort of way, "it seems that you've just won your school's creative writing award for the story you wrote."

"Really?" I asked. I was shocked, but relieved I was going to live to fight crime for another day.

"Ms. Shanahan loved your story so much that she quickly passed it around to all the other teachers at your school, and they decided that you were the winner. Then, I guess your principal got a hold of it and is submitting it for a national writing competition for young people about your age. He thinks you have a good shot at winning that, too!" Dad explained proudly.

"Wow," I exclaimed, barely able to contain my excitement.

As Mom and Dad both gave me a big hug, I knew my Superhero training was starting to pay off, just like Captain Breakthrough had said it would.

"The New Gnu" *ended up being much more than just a short story written on wide-lined paper. My story won many awards, and as a youngster, I reveled in the*

recognition.

I remember how proud I felt when Dad congratulated me for using my mind and imagination so well in my writing. For the first time, I realized I had a talent for writing. Dad had always taught me to learn as much as I could, find my strengths, and then focus on them.

Although it was a simple story that I had created from the experience with my Dad, the clever metaphor behind the tale had triggered an important stage of my growth. Of course, as an eight-year-old, I had no idea that was happening at the time. I only knew that I felt empowered by the successes I enjoyed from my writing, and how it made me feel. Looking back, I know Dad recognized that. Captain Breakthrough was consuming my conscious mind, but I now realize what a big impact Dad was having on my subconscious mind at the same time.

BREAKTHROUGH SUCCESS TIP #3

Focus your attention beyond the problem.
The solution is where the fun begins!

"THE WORLD WILL NOT BE DESTROYED BY THOSE WHO
DO EVIL, BUT BY THOSE WHO WATCH THEM
WITHOUT DOING ANYTHING."

ALBERT EINSTEIN

— Chapter 4 —
Turning On Your Internal Super Magnet

It was a delightful spring day, and although Captain Breakthrough was virtually always "on call," the situation with Dr. Fear had seemed to quiet down over the last couple of weeks, so Breakthrough was taking time to clear his mind, and get some much needed rest. His mind was still focused on finishing the machine he set out to build in a massive effort to not only combat Dr. Fear's diabolical Robotic Thought Vacuum, but eliminate him completely. He knew he would have to rest up for the ensuing battle.

After rescuing a stray cat from a quiet neighborhood tree, and wiping the tears of joy from a little girl's face, Captain Breakthrough again took flight, thinking to himself about how great it was to be a Superhero. As he drifted carelessly through the clouds, he reflected back on his school days at the Academy. He had majored in community service and universal law enforcement. Some of the lessons he learned from his Academy roommate, who had specialized in the marketing aspects of being a Superhero, entered his thoughts. Captain Breakthrough's business was thriving. He was giving back in terms of money and time.

"Reciprocity feels so good," he said to himself, softly.

He began thinking of ways he could improve his performance and his business. He even considered bringing other Superheroes into his team, so he could develop a Superhero consulting practice that he could later franchise on a global scale. Lost in business thoughts, he was quickly distracted by a thunderous crash just below him.

Immediately descending from the clouds, Breakthrough took long, deep breaths as he felt the drop in altitude apply pressure to his head. As he cleared the cloud cover, he saw the source of the terrible sound. It was a car accident, and it didn't look encouraging.

Captain Breakthrough quickly took control of the frightening scene he had just discovered. Immediately, he suspected that it was a result of fearful thoughts being broadcast by Dr. Fear and his evil machine.

The attitude Breakthrough displayed was inspiring. It was reflected not only in what he did, but how he went about his work.

"We will get through this...I know what to do!" Breakthrough quickly assured.

Fear began to spread wildly among the people on the scene. Captain Breakthrough knew he had to act quickly, and with decisiveness, in order to save the lives of the car's occupants.

A crowd had gathered directly around the wreckage, and everyone was in shock. Captain Breakthrough was quick to console the people.

"Success is 10% what happens to you, and 90% how you react to it," he assured.

Immediately, comfort showed on their faces, as they listened to his words, and saw his enthusiasm.

"I'm here to help you . . . there's no need to fear!" he said to the trapped victims. Captain Breakthrough found strength, as he always did, not in physical super powers, but in his enthusiastic and optimistic approach to any circumstance, regardless of how dire it seemed on the surface.

He ripped off the bent, mangled, barely recognizable passenger-side doors, and pulled a woman and child from the car. Remarkably, their injuries were nominal, but their minds were racing with fearful thoughts. He could almost feel them. Breakthrough couldn't see fuel leaking visibly from the car, but flames had started in the engine compartment, so he knew time was limited. In order to buy more time to get all the injured out of the flaming vehicle, Captain Breakthrough once again thought quickly, and acted decisively. He stripped the flame retardant cape from his neck to stamp out the flames, which were now roaring from the engine compartment.

Once the flames were contained, he rushed to the other side of the car and proceeded to rip the remaining doors from their hinges. He pulled the third victim from the driver's seat, who wasn't wearing a seat belt, and

appeared to be in the worst physical condition.

After the passengers and driver were carefully carried from the wreckage to the perceived safety of the roadside, Captain Breakthrough realized that the paramedics had not arrived on the scene to assist.

Breakthrough could sense that Dr. Fear was lurking nearby, in order to watch his creation unfold. Captain Breakthrough knew that Dr. Fear liked to prey on weakened mental states. He was also keenly aware that Fear was easily able to instill his will on a mind in this state, in an attempt to gain ultimate control.

The driver who had not been wearing his seat belt was in the worst condition. Right before Breakthrough's eyes, the wounded man was allowing Dr. Fear to suck the life from him, thus putting him in a state of utter despair. Captain Breakthrough knew he had to go straight to the man's mind.

It was time for Captain Breakthrough to dig deep, and begin saying anything and everything positive he could think of to the man, before Dr. Fear and his evil Thought Vacuum took complete control over his mind. Breakthrough softly approached the wounded man and smiled enthusiastically. It was a genuine, confident smile that spread from one ear to the other. He spoke to the man in a soothing voice.

"Sir, I know how you must feel right now experiencing all of this, but everything is going to be okay. The medics are on their way." He told him calmly and confidently.

"Fortunately, I can see that you are in great physical condition, and you *will* overcome this trauma. What is your name?" he continued. The victim was conscious enough to hear, and although he clearly didn't want to listen to this banter, he replied to the kneeling man with the blue cape.

"I'm Dan," he said in a weak voice.

"I'm right here with you, Dan; take my hand," said Captain Breakthrough. His cape was blackened on one side from the chars burned into the fabric. The black flakes wafted away in the spring breeze, as Captain Breakthrough placed the cape onto the man's body. The deep, royal blue lining on top covered the man, virtually unblemished.

Then, with a confident voice and an encouraging squeeze of the man's hand, Breakthrough reassured the man once more.

"You're going to be fine, Dan, I promise you. You must believe that, and stay with me. It's time for you to fight."

As he continued in dialogue with the man, Captain Breakthrough felt the abominable presence of Dr. Fear drawing closer. He had arrived to intensify his efforts in luring this victim into hopeless thought. This was one blatant circumstance when Dr. Fear's machine was no longer needed. The man's mental state began to deteriorate rapidly. Dr. Fear was in control. Breakthrough saw the expression on the man's face turn to terror as the words rang out from Fear's mouth, now kneeling by his side.

"Your life will never be the same, just give up," Dr. Fear's unharmonious, frightening voice whispered.

"If you survive, you will live a life of pain and suffering forever more. Just accept your fate."

In his weakened state, Dan's mind was beginning to accept Dr. Fear's words as true. The foul odor emanating from Fear's mouth literally made Dan feel weaker. Dan turned his head to the side, in an effort to avoid the offensive smell dripping off of every word Fear uttered. Captain Breakthrough realized that Dr. Fear's gruesome qualities were worsening.

"No, don't listen to him, you have everything to live for Dan," Captain Breakthrough continued.

"Your wife and kids need you! You need to hold on to your positive attitude and enthusiasm for life!" he encouraged. Captain Breakthrough could see that the life force was draining out of the man. Dr. Fear had slithered up behind Dan and wrapped his crooked hands over his shoulders.

This was going to be a direct face-off with Dr. Fear, and Breakthrough knew it! He had to figure out a way to lure Fear away from the accident scene. He had to create a diversion.

Captain Breakthrough and Dr. Fear kneeled on either side of the man.

Both were struggling to win the man's will. Suddenly, Captain Breakthrough had an epiphany. *I know Dr. Fear preys on the weak,* Breakthrough thought to himself. *So I need to create a diversion…one that Fear will think involves MANY people in a weakened state. This is the only way I can get him to leave Dan, so I can help him regain the strength of his positive mental attitude,* his thoughts continued.

Captain Breakthrough stood to his feet, threw back his cape, and looked down at the wounded man. Dr. Fear paid no mind to Breakthrough's gestures.

"There is a possible calamity I must deal with downtown," Breakthrough directed his comment directly toward Dan, with a subtle wink. He kneeled once more, and grabbed the man's hand. With piercing confidence and an almost coded voice, Breakthrough spoke.

"I wish I could stay to help you further, Dan, but I have a sworn oath to help everyone who needs me. I shall return."

By the strangely unique way Breakthrough had grabbed his hand, Dan knew the renowned Superhero had a plan. Even with Fear still kneeling by his side, murmuring words of discouragement, Dan had a sudden, knowing sense that he would be alright. His mind began to embrace the thought that he would recover, and become a better man because of it.

Captain Breakthrough then took his usual three skip-steps forward, and lurched into flight. The plan was simple. The largest building in the city's downtown area, which towered more than 120 stories, and had more than 14,000 businesses running within its many walls, needed to be "in danger". He quickly proceeded to evacuate the building, without Dr. Fear's knowledge. He could use the vacant building to get Fear to think that the nearly 120,000 employees working within it were in danger, and in a frantic state of despair.

After Captain Breakthrough had everyone in the building safely evacuated and out of sight, he grabbed the cornerstone of the building and began to shake the foundation of the large structure with all of his might. He applied just enough pressure to break windows and give it the look of a building that was about to crumble. With deep grunts and veins protruding from his biceps, Breakthrough accomplished his objective. He would rectify the situation later, but the building looked as if it were in shambles.

Then he took flight, immediately returning to the scene of the car accident. As he descended, he could hear an ambulance's sirens in the distance. He knew he needed to hurry in order to covertly let Dr. Fear know about the large building's apparent disaster.

Breakthrough quickly made his way over to Dan. Dr. Fear was still hard at work, bombarding the man with his venomous lies.

"I'm sorry for being so long, Dan," Captain Breakthrough said.

"The Continental Building downtown has suffered massive damage. Many people are trapped and countless numbers are injured," he continued in a way that was sure to get Dr. Fear's attention.

As quickly as he had arrived, Dr. Fear immediately got up and scurried away. He said nothing to anyone, and slithered away like a snake in the night. Breakthrough knew where he was going, but also, that it would prove to be futile. This was exactly what Captain Breakthrough had hoped.

The extra time with Dan, before the paramedics finished their work was all that Captain Breakthrough needed. He continued on, with words of encouragement and, more importantly, gave the man his enthusiastic support.

Weeks later, the driver, who hadn't been wearing his seatbelt, heard about Captain Breakthrough doing a book signing at a local book store. He wanted to shake the Superhero's hand, and thank him personally for giving him the courage to overcome Dr. Fear's grasp, so he could continue being a loving husband and father.

The line was long, as anticipated, because Captain Breakthrough's popularity was growing at an alarming rate, as happiness and positivity had begun to gain a slight upper hand against Fear's diabolical scheme. After rehearsing everything he wanted to say to the Superhero as he waited over forty-five minutes in line, Dan finally approached the table where Captain Breakthrough sat.

"I was involved in that horrible car accident from several weeks ago. If it wasn't for the positive things you said to me that day, I'm sure I would have died," Dan said, thankfully.

"Not from my physical injuries, but from giving up in my mind. Instead, I've recovered almost entirely. Even though I still deal with the after effects of the blow to my head, I have so much to thank you for, Mr. Breakthrough. Now I feel like I have the power within me to overcome ANYTHING, even the symptoms I still have from my brain injury!" he continued, with pride and enthusiasm.

"One thing I learned from this entire situation, thanks to you, is that as long as I control my own mind, I have the power to do anything," Dan continued.

"I also know what you did with that building, and when you donated your own money and time to not only repair the damage you caused, but also renovate it, I was amazed," Dan said, admiringly.

"You went far above and beyond your responsibilities as a Superhero, Mr. Breakthrough. I can't begin to thank you enough. You're a good man."

It was another emotionally charged day for me. I had spent more than five hours at the hospital with my wife, volunteering our time to aid the families of comatose patients.

Even after years of studying human behavior, and the root causes of how people become successful, it still fascinated me just how powerful the mind is. I knew that, even in an unconscious state, these people were still alive mentally. They needed some mental reinforcements, someone with a great attitude and enthusiasm for life, who could talk to their minds. I was just the guy for the job.

Most of the families would gladly let me spend some

time with their loved ones. Many families welcomed the much needed break from their vigil. I would offer the families signed copies of my books as I got to know them better, and would listen to stories about the patients.

The staff always wondered why I enjoyed spending my volunteer time with people who were unconscious, but when I tried to explain the power of the subconscious mind, they looked at me like I had three heads. So I stopped trying to explain why, and just went happily about my work.

Being in a coma, as I came to learn, was the subconscious mind trying to escape from some kind of fear. As I had learned from my Dad, success in anything was all a result of my RESPONSE to what happened to me, not just the circumstances of 'what' happened to me.

Before I went in to speak with my new friend, James, who had been in coma for just over a week, I spent some time with his parents and sister. They had been at the hospital twenty-four hours a day since his car accident. This was my opportunity to go above and beyond my call.

What would Captain Breakthrough say right now? I thought to myself. Then I remembered that as long as I began with an enthusiastic attitude, the words would flow naturally.

After a brief visit, I encouraged the family to take a break. A smile formed on my face, and I proceeded to talk with James alone...to tell him he was completely safe. To let him know he had many friends, and that he was very loved. I was lucky enough to always feel that way growing up...

Reveling in the glory that I had been receiving over my creative writing assignment, I was more focused on my chief aim of becoming Captain Break-through than ever before.

"Maybe someday, I can *write a story* about my experiences with Captain Breakthrough!" I said to Dad.

"That's right, Son; I think that sounds like a *fantastic* idea! This is where your journaling will come in handy. If you spend just a little time each day journaling about your experiences and feelings about things, then you can go back later and use your notes to do *just* that: write your book about all the lessons of Superhero Success™ and Captain Breakthrough," Dad suggested with enthusiasm, as he pumped his fist in my direction.

"You can do *anything* you want to do, Son…remember that!" he continued.

It was Friday night, and I knew the next day, Captain Breakthrough was going to be on again. I could barely contain my excitement, and Dad knew it.

"So, are you learning some valuable lessons from Captain Breakthrough, Gordy?" Dad asked.

"Oh yeah, Dad, I feel like a Superhero *already*, in my mind!"

"Well you know that's where it all starts, Son, so you're doing fine. You're well on your way to becoming a Superhero!" Dad stated.

"But I don't even have an *official* shield," I said, disappointed.

"Well, I think this is a perfect reward for you using your creative mind for positivity, Son. You've shown you do have a true positive mental attitude, like Captain Breakthrough. I'll stop by the store tomorrow on the way down to the hospital and get you one…an 'official' one," Dad offered.

Immediately I felt an explosion building inside of me. I couldn't contain my excitement, and Dad knew it.

"Here's what you need to do," Dad said covertly, as he looked from side to side.

"Go to bed, so your mind is completely fresh for tomorrow, but I want you to think of every possible way this shield is going to help you. Let your imagination run WILD tonight, and tomorrow, I bet you'll get the upper hand on Dr. Fear and his automated mind control thingy," Dad said, not realizing he didn't have the right name.

"Daaaad, it's the Robotic Thought Vacuum!" I corrected.

I went to my bedroom and followed Dad's advice, with my thoughts running wild.

"Tomorrow, Dr. Fear is TOAST!" I said to Jack.

Jack yawned, and soon after, I went to bed.

The morning came quickly. I still had to fill my stomach, feed Jack, and prepare my soon-to-be complete uniform and handmade shield for today's mission against Dr. Fear. I carefully gathered the ingredients for my internal anti-fear repellent, which I liked to drink just before Captain Breakthrough began his mission every Saturday. Mom insisted on referring to it as Ovaltine®, but she didn't understand just how powerful Dr. Fear was. No precaution was too great.

It was still a while before my favorite show started. I had to stay active.

I went into Dad's office with my full glass, and a proclamation.

"I think Dr. Fear is getting stronger, Dad, especially now that his Robotic Thought Vacuum is really causing people to be scared," I said.

"I need to stay strong."

"Good thinking 'Breakthrough,' you're doing a great job!" Dad encouraged, as he continued to look at some papers.

"Don't drink too much...lunch will be ready soon, and I think Mom is going to fix some special Positivity sandwiches made from your favorite lunch meat before we go to the hospital."

"PERFECT! This will give me the energy I need to stay alert AND the repellant will provide added protection against Dr. Fear," I said, as I placed my empty glass with a thump.

Then it hit me.

"Dad, I gotta figure out how to get ALL the money in the world!"

"Why is that, Son? What would you do with all the money in the world?" Dad asked rhetorically, yet anxious for my reply.

"Because with all the money in the world, I'd be able to build MY machine to annihilate Dr. Fear and his Robotic Thought Vacuum, especially now he's gone *national* with it," I demanded.

"I've gotta start treating this like a business, Dad, just like Captain Breakthrough does, and stop Fear before he takes over the world."

"But Son, we've..."

"I know, Dad..." I interrupted. Dad smiled.

"But, if I had all the money in the world, I could also give back more."

Still smiling, Dad replied, "Very good, Gordy...I'm proud of you."

"I know how important giving is, Dad. Even Captain Breakthrough talks about repri...repro..." I began to stutter.

"What do you call it, Dad?" I asked.

"You mean reciprocity?"

"Yeah, yeah, that! So I'd have that on my side, and I'd ALSO be able to build all the *advanced* tools needed to stop Dr. Fear!"

"Success is not about how much money you can acquire, Son. Money is just one measuring stick for success. Money is important...necessary in most cases, but it's mostly a ruler, or measurement, of how well you're doing for the goals you've chosen," Dad said, philosophically.

"However, you must keep in mind, money will never buy things that are essential to your happiness like PEACE of mind. In other words, Son, true contentment can only come from positive thoughts about money and the experiences it provides, and not from the money itself. Whether you're an independent Superhero, or a Superhero that works for someone else, it doesn't matter," Dad said, instructionally.

"So, your positive mental attitude is what attracts the things you want, and if a lot of money is what you want, then you have to know PRECISELY what experience you want that money to provide . . . then when you believe it, 'wholeheartedly,' and your goal is an honest, worthwhile one, then you'll achieve it. Right?"

This was one of those questions that really only had one answer, so I didn't quite know why Dad asked it , but I gave a resounding, confident answer.

"That's RIGHT!"

After flying back to the kitchen to dump my glass in the sink, I was ready. The show was about to start.

Now fully prepared for today's mission, with Jack by my side, and in our usual positions on the floor in front of the television, the show had begun. The exciting music that began every episode seemed to be affecting me today more than usual. My fists were clenched.

"It's going to be a good one today, Jack…I can FEEL it!" I told my fluffy sidekick.

My heart was pounding as this episode came to an end. This was the first episode where I realized that being a Superhero had many complexities. *This isn't just a career; it's a business!* I said to myself. Then I turned to Jack and spoke aloud.

"Being a successful superhero requires mastery of a lot of different things… we have a lot of work to do!"

Once again, Dad magically appeared in the room within seconds of the show coming to an end, and once again, I began to wonder if he was one of Dr. Fear's "Mongers" incognito, sent to suck the life from me somehow.

"He always seems to just *know* when the show ends, Jack…how does he *do* that?!" I whispered.

"How was this week's mission, Son?" Dad asked, in some sort of spaceship Commander's tone.

Sensing that he already knew what happened, I hesitated for a moment, but then my excitement got the better of me.

"Dad, you won't believe what Captain Breakthrough did today. He saw this car wreck and he RIPPED the doors from the hinges to save everyone. SO awesome!" I said, with adulation.

"Then Captain Breakthrough shook this *entire* building to lure Dr. Fear away from the people that were hurt, so he couldn't suck the life from them!"

"Sounds to me like Captain Breakthrough's 90/10 philosophy," Dad replied.

As I was trying to remember what the heck Dad was talking about, he continued.

"When Captain Breakthrough talks about PMA, it's true about the percentages, Son. So, when something happens to you that makes you feel bad, angry, sad, or even excited, your outcome will be based on how you respond. Does that make sense to you?"

"I *think* so…" I said, with some hesitance.

"Captain Breakthrough always says, 'Life is only 10% what happens to you and 90% how you respond to it,' right?"

I nodded in agreement.

"So, if you really want to put the odds of Superhero Success® in your favor, then make sure you adjust your thoughts *now*. *That way* 90% of what "happens" to you are things you really want. If 90% of your response is aimed toward 90% good stuff, then you're going to grow up to be a really happy Superhero!"

There was silence, as I thought about what Dad said. I had a suspicion he was trying to bring my distaste for fractions into my lesson, but I listened anyway as he continued.

"So, when Captain Breakthrough was saving those people in the car wreck, he not only exercised the 90/10 philosophy, but he also went way above and beyond the call of duty, Son. That's an important lesson. It's actually a law of Superhero Success®."

"How many more laws are there for me learn, Dad?" I asked, excitedly.

"You still have a long way to go, but you're coming along right on course; just like I thought you would…you're very smart," Dad said, with his usual wink.

"How 'bout we talk more about it later? Your mother and I have to go down to the hospital to do some volunteer work. Aunt Bev is going to come over and spend some time with you and Jack while we're gone," he said.

I knew this was code for 'I had to spend time with a babysitter.'

"Can't I go with you?" I pleaded.

With a look of consideration toward my plea, he paused.

"Hmmm…you know, I think this would be a great time for you to join us. You can spread some of your positivity to some sick people we help down there."

"Really?!" I asked, excited.

"That sounds like just the job for Captain Breakthrough and me. Dr. Fear likes to sneak up on people that are in a weakened state, and I can SAVE them from getting the life sucked out of them through his Robotic Thought Vacuum."

Although I was disappointed that Dad couldn't talk to me right then and there about how many more laws of Superhero Success® there were, I knew we would address it later. I was really excited about my first trip to the hospital.

"Sure, I think you're ready for it, and…after all…you're *now* at the next stage of your Superhero development," Dad said, in a way that made me feel proud.

"How do you think your help would provide the most impact in their lives, Son?" he followed.

He caught me a bit off guard with the remark because, initially, I had simply imagined showing up with my cape and providing them with a super powerful breakthrough speech, just like Captain Breakthrough did. I envisioned it would inspire them so they could break through any obstacle with ease, if they wanted to.

After what seemed like an eternity, but what was really only about six or seven seconds, I responded with confidence and pride.

"Let's bring them all CAPES, and I'll teach them how to think BIG and to focus on what they want more than ANYTHING else . . . just like you taught me, Dad!" I said, with confidence.

"And we can find out how bad they really WANT to get better."

I smiled and stuck my chest out, concluding that my thinking was a Pulitzer Prize winning idea to help these unfortunate people. Then Dad hit me with another remark that forced me to have to think again.

"What if they need more than that, Son? Remember, some of these people are terminally ill, and are overtaken with so much fear that they've literally put themselves into a state of giving up," Dad explained. He did it in such a way that it both scared me and filled me with pity. I looked at Jack, and wondered what he was thinking.

"In other words, Son, most of these people have lost hope. They've lost their dreams. And this is why your mom and I, as well as several other people, volunteer our time. We understand that it's going to take a lot of repetitive imagination, concentration, and positive thoughts to help them feel better."

I didn't know what to say.

"Go take care of Jack , Son, and let's go. We have an 'official PMA Shield' to get," Dad said, as he waved his hand for me to get ready.

"Don't forget the video camera, Sweet Pea…" Dad said lovingly to Mom.

"I want to make sure we get some of this recorded to motivate our students," he continued.

Students?! I quickly thought to myself.

I hadn't been questioning it, but now I was getting suspicious again.

Why are they inviting me to come with them to the hospital now? Hmmm... I thought to myself.

I had always assumed that my parents had a business of some kind, because they were always talking about their members, or their students.

My thoughts began to race as I wondered if Mom and Dad were indeed covert operatives for Dr. Fear. I quickly thought maybe the hospital thing was a lure to trick me and maybe their minds had been overtaken by The Robotic Thought Vacuum. I was convincing myself that they were falling prey to the dastardly ways of Dr. Fear's mental grip.

I continued to argue with myself. My mind began to think through all the possibilities, just like Dad had always taught me to do. He taught me to examine my thoughts for accuracy to see if my thoughts were working for, or against, me.

"If they were under the influence of Dr. Fear, their sole mission would be to apprehend my mind through covert, incognito tactics. If this IS the case, then this is a masterful piece of work they are doing on me," I went on, preaching to Jack.

"We'll have to stay alert in case it's true, Jack. I'll have to do some more investigating, to make sure they're on the side of truth and justice. We have to make sure that they are in Captain Breakthrough's alliance."

On the way to the hospital, I was laser focused on obtaining my official shield, as Dad had promised. Dad obviously had a somewhat different focus.

"What does education mean to you, Son?"

My mind was was filled with thousands of television screens all playing out different battles with Dr. Fear. All I could muster in response to his question was a soft, "I dunno Dad..."

Seemingly unfazed by my lack of enthusiasm toward his question, he continued.

"Education comes in various forms, but the education I want you to focus

on is earning your CBA degree."

"What? What's CBA stand for Dad? I never heard of that before..." I replied, with growing interest, pausing the television screens in my mind.

"Do you have your journal with you? Remember to keep it with you at all times. That way, your mind knows that you have a place to keep important ideas and it will send you more of them," he instructed.

"Got it right here!" I exclaimed, as I ripped the journal out of my Captain Breakthrough backpack.

"Excellent work; now write these words." Dad continued.

"CONCEIVE

BELIEVE

ACHIEVE"

Mom spelled out the words for me, and I wrote down the letters. Then she took my journal and wrote beside each word:

"YOUR THOUGHTS

WITH ALL YOUR HEART

YOUR SUCCESS"

"I always tell you, Son, that you become what you think about," Dad said with a grin.

Prying my thoughts away from scenes of battle with Dr. Fear for a moment, I became concerned.

"Dad, besides becoming Captain Breakthrough, I think about apple fritters a LOT. Could I become a giant apple fritter?" I immediately became somewhat excited, as I entertained the thought of just how cool the possibilities of THAT would be.

"Yes, that's right, you're well on your way to becoming a piping hot apple fritter!" Dad said sarcastically.

After seeing Mom roll her eyes, we all had a good, hard, belly laugh.

"You know, you can earn your CBA degree in anything you want," Dad encouraged.

"Conceive your dreams and believe in them wholeheartedly...then you will achieve your success."

"Is this like an MBA?" I questioned, proud of myself that I even knew that term.

Dad, looking a bit surprised, replied.

"No, with a CBA, you create the topics that you study based on what you are most passionate about, not what someone else wants you to study. That way, your studies will never become boring, because you are learning more about what you already enjoy. Also, you never have to take any tests, and you can be in class whenever you want!"

"Sounds great to me, Dad!" I said, now at full attention.

"A formal education can be an amazing experience to help you in getting where you want to go in life, if that's what you choose. However, a CBA will insure that you reach your dream destination."

"Dad, there's the store!" I exclaimed loudly from the backseat.

As the car pulled into the parking a lot of the local shopping mall, Dad concluded with his final instruction to me.

"Son, be mindful of your thoughts. Because, whether you think you can do something or you think you can't, you are going to be right, 100% of the time," he said, looking back at me in the rear-view mirror.

After spending more than an hour enthusiastically sharing stories of my days brainstorming alongside Captain Breakthrough with James, there was no movement from his body at all. But I knew he was listening.

My new friend had a long journey ahead, but based on what his family shared with me, I had a hunch that he would make it through this, as long as he was constantly fed positive, encouraging words. Since I was only at the hospital every other Saturday, when I didn't have speaking engagements, I told his family just how important this practice was.

The stories I told of my days with Captain Break-

through got me so inspired that I called my dad on the way home. We talked about how we had each spent the day, and reminisced about our experiences with Captain Breakthrough.

During that conversation, I realized, for the first time, that Dad had always been watching the shows from another room, so he'd know which lessons to teach me each week. I realized that, although at the time, I had somehow thought he was a covert operative under the control of Dr. Fear, in fact, he was really my own, personal, Captain Breakthrough.

With a tear in my eye as I hung up the phone, my wife came up from behind me and put her hand on my shoulder. She reminded me how many people I had helped through my many books and speeches…then she softly reminded me that life is only 10% what happens, and 90% how I respond to it.

BREAKTHROUGH SUCCESS TIP #4

Be so enthusiastic about life that people look at you funny!
You'll be amazed at how exhilarating this is.

"THERE IS LITTLE DIFFERENCE IN PEOPLE, BUT THAT LITTLE DIFFERENCE MAKES A BIG DIFFERENCE. THE LITTLE DIFFERENCE IS ATTITUDE. THE BIG DIFFERENCE IS WHETHER IT IS POSITIVE OR NEGATIVE."

W. CLEMENT STONE

— Chapter 5 —
The Value Of Failing Successfully

Seething over Captain Breakthrough's diversion and trickery in the staged collapse of the famous Continental Building, Dr. Fear vowed to do whatever it took to beat Breakthrough, and dominate the minds of all mankind.

"They will all be MINE, and I will be able to orchestrate the workings of the entire world, toying with people like puppets on a string," he cackled, rubbing his gnarled hands furiously.

Now, with the kinks ironed out of his Robotic Thought Vacuum, legions of loyal "Fear Mongers" were leading his cause. Dr. Fear was sure his attempt to rule the world would be victorious. In his mind, it was just a matter of time.

What he didn't realize during this devious planning was that he was, in essence, exercising many laws of success, but for the wrong purposes. The mind is very powerful, and Dr. Fear had mastered the flow of his thoughts. However, like many failed dictators before him, he had yet to learn that his use of the laws of success for an evil purpose was doomed from the start. The essential ingredient of positivity is the catalyst for all successful endeavors.

Captain Breakthrough had disappeared from public view, which alarmed some, but many people were already living in a state of fear. Those who had been deeply affected by the Robotic Thought Vacuum were oblivious to his disappearance. Breakthrough had found himself getting disgusted and short-tempered as he continued to endure sleepless nights spent pondering a solution to the Robotic Thought Vacuum. But, as he continued to focus on the solution instead of the problem, Captain Breakthrough began to notice that he was developing a higher tolerance level for dealing with negative people; he was exercising a sense of self-control he had not ever experienced before.

He was so intrigued by this experience that, he began to research exactly what it was in the human brain that triggered the feeling of self-control (or lack of it). With much study he found that, not surprisingly, self-control, like all the core principles of success in life, is a conscious decision, triggered from subconscious programming.

After taking a week of solitude to carefully consider this new information about self-control, he wondered about all the different areas of life where self-control could have an impact. Breakthrough fully understood the power of saving, as he was both punctual and habitual with his retirement investing, and he realized that this, too, was a form of self-control.

Self-control is very powerful... he thought to himself, *...I have the power to program my mind to do ANYTHING I want,* his thoughts continued.

"Now I need to direct my self-control to save up all my energy to defeat Fear once and for all!" he declared, shouting aloud.

"I need to develop an organized plan for the ultimate destruction of Dr. Fear and his Robotic Thought Vacuum," Captain Breakthrough continued aloud.

"I've got to get the Supercharged Mind Expander deployed!" he ordered, anonymously.

He emerged back into the public scene a few days later, performing his usual acts of kindness, which were a part of his daily responsibility as a Superhero. He was now refocused, due to the fact he took the time to organize a plan to annihilate Dr. Fear. He felt confident about it. In fact, he was more focused than ever before. The time alone had given him the opportunity to reflect on his victories, and also his failures.

His victories were easy to learn from. But more importantly, through assessing his failures, he strengthened his belief in himself, which fueled him to make the necessary corrections. The knowledge he gained from these reflections provided him with the persistence needed to overcome the many challenges and obstacles that he would face during not only his lifelong journey, but his upcoming battle against Dr. Fear.

Dr. Fear was now more vengeful than ever. He acted on his rage, turning the majority of the full effects of the Robotic Thought Vacuum away from the masses, and solely toward his nemesis, Captain Breakthrough. At the scene of their last meeting, it was Captain Breakthrough who had stolen Dr. Fear's victim away, from right under his nose!

As he continued through his day, still contemplating how he would complete the development of his machine to battle Fear, he began to feel himself getting weak. "What is Fear up to?!" Captain Breakthrough said feebly. "My only hope is to maintain my self-control." The numbingly powerful effects of Dr. Fear's Robotic Thought Vacuum were starting to affect Captain Breakthrough, and he felt powerless.

In a feeble mental state, which started to affect his physical strength, Breakthrough gathered every ounce of energy he had left in his body, and flew back to his lair. It was time. The release of his Supercharged Mind Expander, his only hope against Fear's Robotic Thought Vacuum, had to happen quickly.

Displaying complete self-control, Captain Breakthrough gathered the quickly waning energy left in his body, crawled to his desk, and reclined back in his chair. There he began to focus on the end result—he would annihilate Fear completely, and create a confident society capable of breaking through any challenge, NEVER to be governed by fear again!

Captain Breakthrough had been laser focused on destroying Dr. Fear for months, but Fear wasn't going away...HE WAS ACTUALLY EXPANDING AND BECOMING MORE POWERFUL! Up to this point, Breakthrough had only been able to deflect Dr. Fear, but his aim was to obliterate him forever. He had to think accurately.

Breakthrough's biggest breakthrough yet – the computerized high frequency contraption he was designing to combat Fear's Robotic Thought Vacuum – had come to a standstill for months. Aware of the upgrades Dr. Fear had made to his dastardly Robotic Thought Vacuum, Captain Breakthrough had considered all of the possibilities for his own grand machine. The initial prototypes of The Supercharged Mind Expander were that of

a computerized robot, with high frequency speakers, which could send out positive messages at the flick of a switch. Still reeling from his own experience from the Robotic Thought Vacuum, Breakthrough knew that it was going to take more than positive affirmations to thwart Dr. Fear, and the latest prototype of the Supercharged Mind Expander needed work.

Persistent in his quest, he researched long into the night and discovered the highly intricate systems Dr. Fear was utilizing. Now armed with the wickedly powerful technology used to back up Fear's Robotic Thought Vacuum, the matching technology programmed into Captain Breakthrough's Mind Expander was sure to negate its powerful negative effects.

"I will make sure the Supercharged Mind Expander is programmed to withstand ANYTHING that Fear concocts to counteract my amazing device. This machine will fight until the truth and self mastery of everyone's mind PREVAILS!"

Meanwhile, thousands of people were succumbing to Dr. Fear's mass rays of negativity, and having the life sucked right out of them via their thoughts. That was just what Fear wanted!

Soon, Breakthrough faced another obstacle in his aim to destroy Dr. Fear. Captain Breakthrough's Supercharged Mind Expander ended up costing far more than he had ever imagined. Being the public figure he was, Captain Breakthrough was embarrassed by all the publicity he, and the machine, had been receiving from the global news. He was being ridiculed by some, and revered for his efforts by others. Yet, he was unfazed by the people who criticized him, and focused on utilizing his mental muscles to their fullest capacity to exercise self-control, for he knew that he was being tested from many different angles.

Government funding for his machine had been brought to a halt, due to the machine's complicated technology requirements, and the supercharged power needed to run it. Grants and donations to the project had ceased, due to the negative publicity being spun by Dr. Fear and his loyal "Fear Mongers." It looked as though Breakthrough's machine to fight fear and expand mankind's minds would never become a reality.

Although thoughts of doubt and worry occasionally entered Captain Breakthrough's mind, he didn't give these thoughts any power by focusing on them. He knew that thoughts themselves could not affect him, unless he attached meaning to them and gave them his attention. Instead, he focused fully on the belief in his machine, and his hope for mankind. These beliefs led him to trust his instincts, and invest his own money into the project.

"I am thankful that I saved my money and invested wisely," he said in a loud, confident tone.

"Now I will take the action steps necessary to finally make the Supercharged Mind Expander a reality." Captain Breakthrough knew there was still much work to do. All mankind was relying on him to thwart Dr. Fear's efforts. He would have to ensure that the Supercharged Mind Expander was ready for action.

I was exhausted. Physically and mentally, I needed a break. I had spent the last ten days speaking to teenagers about conquering bullies, as well as overcoming other fears and obstacles on the road to success. I had bounced around between various high schools and colleges in the northwest, and now I was finally headed home.

I couldn't have been more satisfied with how things went. In fact, I was elated. I think it was due to the fact that the kids had gotten so excited when I instructed them on how to be guaranteed millionaires by simply practicing self-control, saving, and having an organized plan.

Known for bringing humor to thought-provoking topics in my speeches, I had particular affinity for teenagers. I had a talent for knowing just how to open their minds to new ideas and different modes of thinking. As I walked through the airport on my way to my last connecting flight, my mind was filled with memories of all the great kids that had just left an impression on me. Many were filled with vibrant hopes and dreams…they seemed to be almost fearless. Then there were others that were clearly showing signs of walking in the shadow of fear. Although I knew most of them were listening when I spoke, I still found myself hoping that they all had learned something from my speech.

As I walked by a magazine stand, my phone rang. Like a ray of sunshine beaming from my phone, my twin girls' picture popped up. They were eight years old now, but I still stubbornly kept a picture of them at two years old in my phone.

Lost in the sound of their voices, excited from the knowledge that I was almost home, I suddenly stood frozen in my tracks. I found myself in front of a store that sold classic, vintage toys. I stared through the window while I finished the quick chat with my girls. As I hung up the phone, I stood glued to the spot. Almost as though a spotlight were shining down from above...I couldn't believe my eyes. There, illuminated, behind the glass, was a limited edition, mint condition, Captain Breakthrough doll in its original box.

Apparently, I was not the first grown man to have his nose and palms pressed to the display window of this novelty classic toy store. A saleswoman came up to me and, with a polite smile, asked if I had one as a kid. Somehow, I'm sure she knew I did.

Cleverly concealed under his cape was a string - when pulled, the cape would automatically flap in the *air generated beneath it, and he would "speak." I asked her to show it to me. She carefully took the doll out of the box, so I could see that it worked. For the next five minutes, pull after pull, I was mesmerized listening to every positive message Captain Breakthrough had to say.*

They didn't have a Dr. Fear doll, but I had to have Captain Breakthrough to show my girls. My original doll was proudly displayed in my office, but had long since lost the ability to play his motivational sayings. He had been my constant companion since I was eight years old. We had overcome many obstacles together over the years, and he definitely showed the wear a little boy can inflict during his adventures.

Of course, I had more than enough money to pay the hefty price for the vintage doll. Happily lost in thought, I felt like I was flying through the airport. I recalled how important it was more than three decades earlier for me to have a Captain Breakthrough outfit. This memory triggered all the lessons Dad taught me about self-control, and the reason why you need to have an organized plan for saving for the future.

Another episode of Captain Breakthrough had just come to a close.

Now, seeing Dr. Fear more powerful than ever before with his Robotic Thought Vacuum operating at full capacity, I knew I needed a highly organized plan if I was going to save the world. The positive impact I had had on the people at the hospital was still fresh in my mind.

I paced the living room floor with Jack right at my heels. With every abrupt turn, my flowered cape would flap in the air behind me.

"C'mon subconscious…I need your help!" I said aloud, just like Dad had taught me to do when I needed inspiration. Twenty minutes passed, and as I anxiously awaited the ideas I needed - then it hit me.

"I GOT it!" I exclaimed, looking straight at Jack.

"We may not have enough money to construct our own Supercharged Mind Expander yet, Jack, but we do have our *minds*.   We need to think beyond the problem and focus on the *solution,* boy…we need an *organized plan,*" I said, as Jack continued to cling to every word I said.

"I have the official shield, but now I need to iron out the kinks in my uniform…I need to get a *real* uniform with a *real,* flame retardant cape," I continued in a whispering tone of excitement.

"Dad said if I want to be a Superhero like Captain Breakthrough, then I have to really play the part."

I had saved up nearly thirty-five dollars for helping Dad and Mom with various jobs around the house. For every dollar I earned, Dad would take me to the bank to make my usual twenty percent deposit into my savings account. I had no real comprehension of what leverage was, but Dad always told me by depositing this twenty percent of my earnings, I was creating a lot of financial leverage for when I got older.

I kept most of my earnings in my high security, armored, super safe, but Dad and Mom preferred the term piggy bank. It was for global emergencies.

I was hungry, so I headed back to headquarters for some lunch. My sidekick was not far behind.

Mom was preparing another great lunch consisting of Positivity sandwiches, which she knew I loved.

"Dad, I really need to get a new uniform so I can fight Dr. Fear better," I stated abruptly. I went on.

"You told me I'm progressing nicely in my Superhero training, so why can't I have an official uniform to match my new PMA shield?" I asked.

"That's a very good question, Son," Dad said, as he sipped on his lemonade.

"You've been saving up your money, so don't you think it's time to consider investing some of it in your new *official* uniform?" he questioned.

"Investing?" I asked.

"The money you make me invest is in the bank."

"That's the investment money for your future that you shouldn't ever touch, no matter what, until you get older. That is the money that guarantees you'll be rich someday, even if you make some mistakes along the way…and you will," Dad informed.

"The money I'm talking about is your present investment money that you keep in your high security safe," he said, as he shared a smile with Mom.

"But Dad, that's for global emergencies…like if Dr. Fear were to come up with something even more powerful than his Robotic Thought Vacuum!" I pleaded.

"Well, that's a very good point, Son, but remember…we do have Captain Breakthrough helping us out too," Dad affirmed.

"Here's what I think you should do," he continued.

"You've practiced such amazing self-control by saving all that money, I think you should consider using the money to invest in your own, brand new, official Captain Breakthrough uniform to match your shield…"

"But Dad, I don't have enough money for the new official uniform!" I stated sympathetically.

"It costs fifty dollars," I went on, sadly.

Dad glanced quickly at Mom again.

"Well, I tell you what…you've been doing such a good job at saving your money, that your Mom and I would like to float you a loan…the fifteen dollars you're short," Dad offered.

My ears perked up, and I looked at Dad.

"Really?" I said, with a smile.

"Yep, your mom and I will do this for you, but only after you've spent a few days thinking about it, to make sure you want to invest your money in this…. you know how important it is to think things through," Dad said.

As usual, Dad was making me use my mind again.

I had overheard Dad talking to Mom earlier about how important it was that I learn the importance of thinking accurately before making major decisions. This was my life savings, but the new uniform was vital.

I realized that charity from Dad and Mom for a fledgling Superhero needing a new uniform was out of the question. So, after devouring two Positivity sandwiches and a glass of high-energy fear repellant, I was ready for take off.

As Jack and I headed back to the backyard for another adventure, thoughts of my new uniform were at the forefront of my mind. I began to soar through the backyard.

"We're leaving in thirty minutes, Son," Dad announced from the sliding doors that engulfed the back of our house.

I wasn't overly concerned with where we were going on our trip, because I was up for the adventure. There might be more people to save where we were going. Upon finding out this adventure was actually a trip to the mall for Dad to pick up some odds and ends, I was thoroughly disappointed, and demanded to know how long we would be.

"Are we gonna be there long?" I asked, hastily.

"Probably not, Son, but I think it's important you disappear from the house for a while, so you can clear your mind and focus on your game plan for the rest of the day…like Captain Breakthrough does," Dad responded.

I viewed it as a sound plan, and nodded my head with a look of confidence.

As we walked through the mall, I was totally bored, but used the time wisely to continue thinking about my new uniform. At one point, I glanced to one side, where I noticed a crowd beginning to gather in the middle of the mall. It was in an area that had been specifically designed as a kids' play area. The mall provided supervision so kids could play in peace, without being bothered by their parents.

"MEET CAPTAIN BREAKTHROUGH IN PERSON!" the large blue banner with bright yellow letters read.

"Dad, Dad, look, look!" I pleaded, as I pulled on his arm.

Not noticing the crowd, Mom and Dad stopped to see what I wanted. Dad read the sign, told Mom to continue on without us, and dropped a kiss on her cheek. Off we went to see what was going on.

"This is my chance to tell him about everything he's taught me, Dad!" I exclaimed, as I galloped beside him, holding his hand.

"Let's check it out…" Dad said.

I had my bed sheet cape on and PMA Shield with me as we approached the colorful display. It was real. This was my chance to meet my hero, Captain Breakthrough, in the flesh!

"Looks like he's not going to be here for two more weeks, Son..." Dad said as he continued to read the details.

"Yeah, we have to purchase raffle tickets and with each ticket, you get a chance to win time with Mr. Breakthrough himself."

"Captain. It's Captain Breakthrough, Dad, not *mister,*" I said, correcting him.

"Oh...yeah...sorry, uh, Captain...Breakthrough," Dad said, clearing his throat.

"I'll pay for you to have one entry, Son, but if you want to have more than that, you'll have to pay for them on your own. You're going to have to make some serious choices. Do you want to have more chances to meet *Captain Breakthrough* or do you want your new, *official* uniform?" Dad presented.

Faced with this vexing dilemma, I think Dad knew I was a bit confused about what to do.

"You've shown great persistence, Son, in saving your money, so I'm confident that you can do it again if you choose to wait on the uniform and purchase more raffle tickets."

"I'm gonna think about it, Dad" I responded, calmly.

Inside, my heart was racing. The thrill of immediate gratification rushed through my body at the thought of meeting the one, the only, Captain Breakthrough in person.

But I want that official uniform, too... I thought to myself.

As hard as it was for me, I left the decision for later. I knew Mom came to the mall often, so I'd have another chance to purchase more tickets for the raffle if I wanted to.

All the way home, I was fixated on thoughts of the new uniform AND of meeting my idol in person. As soon as I got home, I went immediately to my bedroom to think.

"I don't know what I'm gonna do, Jack. I want both the uniform AND to meet Captain Breakthrough," I confided to my trusty sidekick.

I continued my pursuit of Dr. Fear and his Robotic Thought Vacuum after school the next two days. I had finally decided meeting Captain Breakthrough in person took precedence over the uniform, for now.

The next afternoon, I was in the backyard, with Jack on my chest representing the harmful rays of negativity, when Mom called to me from inside the house.

"Gordy, I'm going to the mall, let's go!" she called.

I grabbed Jack and gave him a big hug. "I'm coming!" I yelled back, as I sprinted toward the sliding doors, bed sheet flapping behind me.

I had to get to my high security, armored, super safe to get my stash. I was planning to take my entire thirty-five dollars and buy thirty-five more chances to meet Captain Breakthrough. I knew the one-on-one time would definitely take me to the next level on my Superhero journey.

I had to be covert, because I was sure Mom and Dad would not approve of this tactic, but my mind was set.

Now, with thirty-five dollars, consisting of mostly coins, bursting out of my pockets, Mom and I set off to the mall.

"Mom, can I go play in the middle while you shop?" I asked, covertly.

Mom walked with me to the play area to make sure I arrived safely. Once I was sure she was out of sight, I went straight to the table where the Captain Breakthrough tickets were being sold.

After purchasing thirty-five new entries to the raffle, I secretly stuffed the tickets in my pockets, so Mom wouldn't see them. I continued to make my way around the indoor playground, saving the other kids from the evil Robotic Thought Vacuum.

It was one more week until the drawing was to be held. It seemed like an eternity. Finally, the day they were notifying the winners of the raffle came around. I was sure it was just a matter of time until I got the call about my victory. I wanted to say something to Mom and Dad, but I couldn't.

As the hours ticked by, the phone remained silent.

Nothing.

"Is everything Okay, Son?" Dad asked, inquisitively.

"Um, yeah, sure Dad…why do you ask?" I asked, tentatively.

"Well, you're usually in your room messin' around with Jack or playing with your Captain Breakthrough doll…"

"Dad, it's *not* a DOLL!" I snapped.

"Err, I mean…fighting crimes of negativity with your business partner Captain Breakthrough," he asserted.

I was freaking out, because I had just invested my entire savings on something I knew Dad wouldn't approve of. Even though Dad did tell me I could make my own choice of what I wanted to do with my money, I knew this was not what he had in mind.

The next day, I woke up scared and disappointed. The reality of the situation hit me. I had not won the chance to meet Captain Breakthrough, and now I had no money in my safe for global emergencies that were bound to happen, now that Dr. Fear's power was rising.

"The Thought Vacuum is going to take us ALL now, Jack!" I said, in a state of panic.

In a near-despair because of my loss, I still desperately wanted to meet my hero in person. It took some sincere prodding on my part, but Mom finally agreed to take me to the mall the day he was going to be there. Although I knew I couldn't meet him personally, I hoped I could at least catch a glimpse of him from a distance and be in his presence.

"Just to be *close* to him, Mom, will do some good. Think of what good all that positivity will *do* for me and my efforts to *save* us from Dr. Fear!" I coaxed.

She agreed to take me, and we went to the mall. It was a madhouse. I was sure Dr. Fear was among us. As I walked into the mall, holding Mom's hand, I was on the lookout for his black cloak.

I know he's here somewhere, I thought to myself, as I scanned for the evil doctor.

We finally made it to the vicinity of the play area, and managed to work our way to within about twenty bicycle lengths from where Captain Breakthrough was about to make his grand appearance. I felt envious of the small handful of kids that were on the stage. They had won the raffle, and were going to spend one-on-one time with Captain Breakthrough after his grand appearance.

"He should be out any minute, Gordy," Mom said, smiling. She knew how much this meant to me, so she moved a little to the side, so I could stand on a wall that had been built to protect some flowers.

"How much longer, Mom?" I asked.

"Ladies and gentleman, boys and girls…get your cameras ready…here he comes…The Superhero of All Superheroes…The Master Of Positivity…The Famous Fear Fighter…The One..The Only….Caaaaaptain Breaaaaaaakthrough!" the announcer called out.

I was frozen. The anticipation was killing me. Then from the right side of the stage an arm with a PMA Shield slowly revealed itself. The audience roared.

Mom looked up at me and smiled as I was jumping on the little wall in excitement.

The arm and shield disappeared momentarily, and then he appeared. It took a moment for my eyes to adjust, but there he was. Rich blue cape, blue gloves and boots, yellow belt, and a big red B on his chest.

My excitement quickly dropped to the pit of my stomach.

"Mom, it's not him!" I demanded.

"It's not him…it's an IMPOSTER!"

I was shocked. I was mortified. There on center stage was a man older than Dad, with a small, but noticeable belly protruding over his belt. His posture was that of a man who had been taken by Dr. Fear.

"We have to go, Mom! Quick!" I exclaimed jumping from the wall.

"It's not him…it's an IMPOSTER! Dr. Fear is among us…we have to go before it's too late!" I pleaded.

Finally, Mom agreed to get me out of there. I don't think she was convinced, but we went straight to the car and headed back home. Little was said in the car, but I knew the presence of impostors was not good.

"The world needs me now MORE THAN EVER!" I said to Mom.

"You're absolutely right, Gordy! Let's go home, so you can get back to work," she replied.

Upon arriving home, I grabbed Jack to update him on the desperate situation.

"There are impostors of Captain Breakthrough everywhere Jack! Right at our own mall!" I exclaimed, in a hair-raising tone.

Knowing that I had depleted all my funds to respond to this global emergency, I was convinced I needed to be prepared for the days of battle sure to come. I had to have a new uniform.

Ignoring thoughts of my previous grounding for the down pillow incident, I immediately went into Mom's closet and took out her flowing red dress.

"I know just the one I need. She bought it for that awards dinner she and dad went to last week. It's just the right color," I said excitedly, as I threw it over my arm.

I proceeded to Dad's closet. I needed yellow. I walked straight to Dad's dresser and pulled out his bright yellow golf shirt.

"This is perfect!" I exclaimed. It was the shirt that Dad had worn when he shot a hole in one about a year prior.

"Now for the cape," I said quietly to Jack.

I continued to sneak into the living room to continue my work. According to Mom, this room was *only* to be used for special occasions and important functions.

"It can't get any more important than a new cape to withstand Dr. Fear's Robotic Thought Vacuum," I commanded, still in a quiet tone.

"The world NEEDS me!"

I walked to the royal blue curtains Mom had custom made for this room and proceeded to carve out the perfect cape.

"On to the chest logo!" I said, as I stomped over to Mom's dress.

Jack looked on timidly, and I sat down and cut out the form of a B from the middle of the dress.

"Dad always says you have to take risks, so that's what I'm doing, right Jack?" I asked, looking his way.

"And Dad said, too, that failure is all part of my Superhero training, so I'm sure losing the raffle will qualify as a failure in their minds," I continued.

"Anyway, we MUST have a reliable uniform if we expect to prevail against Dr. Fear…Mom and Dad will understand that…right?" I was feeling hesitant.

I still found myself justifying my actions aloud to Jack.

I carefully laid down all the pieces I had just carved out for my new and

improved Captain Breakthrough outfit.

"I'll have to spray it down with some of Dad's clear coat lacquer from the garage so it will retard all flames, too, and then I'll end up with a uniform even more powerful than Captain Breakthrough has," I went on.

"Dad and Mom should be *proud* of me for being so thrifty and using household items to build my uniform anyway," I continued to justify.

After about two hours of intense trimming and gluing, my outfit was nearly complete.

I carefully moved some things around in Dad's dresser, Mom's closet, and in the family room, so the missing pieces wouldn't show too much. With my new uniform I knew I could now adequately combat Dr. Fear.

I headed back to the living room to put on my new unofficial Captain Breakthrough uniform. Before I had a chance to slip on my creation, I immediately sensed Mom standing behind me. She let out the blood curdling rendition of my name that usually meant I had tallied up yet another failure on my path to being a Superhero.

"GOOOOORDY!" Mom said, with exasperation and a bit of anger.

Dad was standing beside her, and he did not look pleased. Still, he gave me the feeling he would at least hear me out.

"I needed a *real* uniform. The world was in *danger*!" I said confidently. Mom looked like she wanted to say something but quickly left the room. Dad motioned for me to follow him into the kitchen.

"But why didn't you just buy the uniform? We told you we would gladly loan you the difference for your uniform from the store..." Dad questioned.

I was silent as I looked at the floor. Knowing that Dad had a way of asking a million questions that eventually got the truth out of me anyway, I decided to fess up.

"I used all my money to buy raffle tickets to see Captain Breakthrough. I didn't win, so I thought it was important to make an outfit because I needed to protect the world," I said, as quickly as I could.

Dad took a long, deep breath before he responded calmly.

"Son, I'm looking at your uniform, and yes you are right, it's one amazing uniform. You did save money, and . . . you had a plan and got organized, and …you were persistent . . .however, you were lacking a key component…self-control."

I still wasn't sure whether I was being punished or if I was being taught one of Dad's *famous* lessons, but I stood there and listened.

"I'm really disappointed in your lack of self-control, Son. You took things that didn't belong to you and destroyed them. What do you think Captain Breakthrough would do in this situation?" Dad asked me.

Knowing he didn't want me to mention a word about combating Dr. Fear, I just stayed quiet.

"Go upstairs to your lair and reflect on your choices, and I'll be up in a few minutes," Dad said.

I quietly went to my bedroom and waited. After a few minutes, the door slowly opened.

"Here's what we're going to do, Son…" Dad began quickly.

"Your Mom and I discussed it, and we decided that, although you showed poor judgment, inaccurate thinking, and lack of self-control in this matter, we're not going to punish you," he went on.

He immediately got my attention. I sat up from the slouched posture I was in.

"Huh?" I questioned.

"We both think this is a perfect time to teach you a valuable lesson in life… after all, part of becoming a Superhero is learning from your mistakes, right?" he asked me, with a wink.

"YES SIR!" I said at full attention.

"For the next year, we're still going to pay your allowance…you still have to work for it around the house…but you have to continue to put your 20% into the bank, then split the rest," he explained.

"Split the rest?" I questioned.

"That's right. You're going to pay 50% back to us to pay for the things you damaged, and the other 50% you're going to donate to a charity…in your name of course," Dad said.

He had kept it short and sweet. All I knew was I had escaped without another prison sentence. I got to keep my outfit, too, but I think that was mostly Mom's idea, in an effort to save their home from further destruction.

On the flight home, I couldn't sleep like I normally did. I just stared at my new Captain Breakthrough doll, thinking of how I could use it in my speeches, and somehow write it off as a business expense. I pulled the string from his back time and time again, until the woman next to me politely asked me to stop.

Now, just staring at the doll, I thought about how thankful I was that Dad taught me how to save at an early age. I thought about the time I spent my entire life savings for a chance to meet the real Captain Breakthrough, and how disappointed I was that he had turned out to be an imposter. In the end, it wound up being one of the most valuable lessons Dad ever taught me, as it paved the way for the success I enjoy today.

Knowing what an impact the Captain Breakthrough cartoon had on me as a kid, I couldn't help but wonder how I could buy the rights and have him inspire a whole new generation of people, just like it did for Dad and I. I even thought about how I could add more characters and inject my own brand of humor into the entire cast, so people all over the world could laugh and learn all at the same time.

My thoughts were really gaining momentum as i imagined how these characters, along with an inspiring message, could entertain millions of people. Then I realized my plane was preparing to land.

I shifted in my seat and started to think about my family, who would be waiting for me at the airport. I knew I was going to need something to justify to my *wife why I had paid so much for a doll…I needed Captain Breakthrough's Supercharged Mind Expander.*

As the plane began its descent to Florida, I started to think about the tour I had just completed. Working with teenagers, I discovered more about myself than I had learned in most of my other presentations, yet I didn't think any of it would have the same effect on me as the Superhero riding home on the plane with me had.

BREAKTHROUGH SUCCESS TIP #5

Don't try to avoid failures. The real failure is
not learning a lesson from them.

"MANY OF LIFE'S FAILURES ARE PEOPLE WHO DID NOT REALIZE HOW CLOSE THEY WERE TO SUCCESS WHEN THEY GAVE UP."

THOMAS EDISON

— Epilogue —

In each week's episode, as the cartoon characters bring to light new challenges, Gordy is persistent in his pursuit of becoming a Superhero, like Captain Breakthrough, and learning the laws of Superhero Success™ that his dad creatively teaches him. Being the brave adventurer, Gordy also continues to find himself in self-created messes as he soars forward in his journey.

With Jack loyally, and sometimes hesitantly, by his side, Gordy continues to grow, along with Captain Breakthrough. What he doesn't yet understand is that what he's learning along the way is setting the stage for a successful future, just as his dad wanted.

As the Saturday morning cartoon goes into each new week, Captain Breakthrough and Dr. Fear proceed to battle against one another in the exciting face-off between fear and a positive mental attitude. New wrinkles present themselves as Captain Breakthrough works diligently to outwit the vindictive mind of Dr. Fear.

Who's going to win this battle to the finish? Will Captain Breakthrough conquer his biggest challenge of all or will Dr. Fear prevail in his diabolical mission to destroy all positivity?

Don't miss the exciting continuation of the battle, and also how Gordy's dad creatively uses it to teach his young son even more about what it takes to achieve the highest levels of success in *Superhero Success*™ Volume II.

Here is a sneak peek at Superhero Success, Volume II...

While Gordy's initiative never lacked, with each passing week, he learns more and his leadership skills continues to grow. What kinds of messes will he get himself into? How will his father teach the importance of unique and specialized knowledge? How will he help young Gordy expect success through action, but always be ready for failure?

Captain Breakthrough finally launches his magnificent Supercharged Mind Expander to combat Dr. Fear's Robotic Thought Vacuum. Will it be enough to finally annihilate fear? Sinister thoughts take the form of organized plans in Dr. Fears mind. What sort of retaliation will he unleash on Captain Breakthrough and the people of the world?

With several strategies up his sleeve, Gordy's dad devises yet another clever plan to help his young son understand the next steps on his journey to becoming a real-life Superhero.

Captain Breakthrough finally learns the root cause of Dr. Fear's motives and enlists the help of a female Superhero he has mentored. Will Breakthrough be able to protect the people and convince Dr. Fear to join him? Or will Dr. Fear continue on his reign of negativity and sinister plot to induce fear on the world?

Don't miss what's next in Volume II of Superhero Success™.

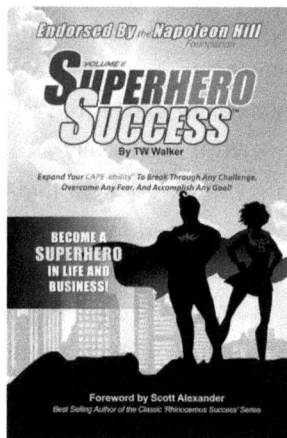

Get my FREE 14-day video training and ebook:
How To Become A Network Marketing Superhero And
Go From Part Time Income To Lifestyle Freedom
www.TWWalker.com

— Superhero Success Action Planner —

Superhero Success™ all starts with a single thought, which is up to you. But it's also dependent on your CAPE-ability®. The level of success you achieve in life or business is all dependent on the level of commitment you have for its attainment. You cannot attain what you cannot first think…from there, you can expand your CAPE-ability® to achieve anything! Once the seed of thought is planted squarely in your mind, the speed at which success finds you is dependent on the level of desire backing up the commitment you make to it. There is a price tag to attaining Superhero Success™, but only you can determine how much it will cost for you. Are you willing to pay the price?

The Action Planner below will help you with the rest of the steps needed to improve your leadership abilities, attain peak performance, and accomplishment of your goals.

Take the time to complete this. You'll be glad you did.

So grab a pencil, strap on your cape, and get ready to SOAR HIGH!

I, _____ ,

(Write Your Name Here)

agree to never let go of the child within myself. I further agree to trust that as long as I am consistently and passionately pursuing an honest and worthwhile goal, then the universe will always respond with exactly with what I need in order to attain it. I agree that anytime a fear of any kind presents itself in my life, I will address it head-on and verbally affirm my goals or look at this sheet. I also understand that achieving Superhero Success™ will not happen overnight, and I will NOT give up trying to break through anything in my path until every goal I set for myself is attained.

_____

(Today's Date)

Chapter 1 – Thinking Like A Superhero

List your top five dreams. Think BIG! You're able to break through anything!

1. _____

2. _____

3. _____

4. _____

5. _____

Daily, I will take time to close my eyes and imagine myself living out each of the above with vivid clarity in each and every detail. I will allow myself to live out the entire experience in my mind until it consumes my daily thoughts.

Chapter 2 – Constructing An Indestructible Cape

List three things that make you feel confident in yourself. You're able to break through anything!

1. _____

2. _____

3. _____

List three decisions you know you need to make that will change everything for you. Anything is possible!

1. _____

2. _____

3. _____

List your top three Power Statements. After you declare them, all you have to do is train your subconscious mind to BELIEVE it!

1.   I am _____

2.   I will _____

3.   I have _____

Daily, I will take time to read aloud the above three Power Statements. I will do this once in the morning when I wake up and once in the evening before going to bed until the feeling of self-confidence within me is strong!

Chapter 3 – Developing X-ray Vision

List three reasons why your dreams are worth breaking through anything to achieve them.

1.   _____

2.   _____

3.   _____

List three positive things you see *beyond* the top three challenges you face in life. This is a tough exercise, so think it through accurately. Remember, you have a cape now…you're able to break through anything!

1.   _____

2.   _____

3.   _____

Daily, I will focus on the solution to my challenges, not the challenges them-selves. *(An exercise for this is to hold your hand in front of you, no more than eight inches away from your face. Now, take your focus off of the hand in order to focus on the scene behind it. You'll find your fingers become transparent. Your hand, in this exercise, represents the problem. Everything behind it is the solution).* Break through anything!

Chapter 4 – Turning On Your Internal Super Magnet

List three things you're *so enthusiastic about* that you do it for the fun and thrill of doing it. Think outside the cape on this one…it can be anything!

1. _____

2. _____

3. _____

Describe three times in your life when nothing more than your positive atti-tude has gotten you things that otherwise you weren't 'qualified' for. Like a promotion, like a new friend, like special treatment, etc. You're powerful…you can break through anything!

1. _____

2. _____

3. _____

Daily, I will wake up with an *attitude of gratitude* and say aloud, "It's going to be a GREAT day because I said so!". Be willing to go the extra mile. Be willing to pay the price. Seek a BREAKTHROUGH every day! Walk. Your. Talk.

Chapter 5 – The Value Of Failing Successfully

List three things you have failed at doing followed by the lesson you learned from each! Until you develop the persistence to break through challenges over and over again, then apply what you learned from it , success will elude you.

Failure: _____

Lesson: _____

Failure: _____

Lesson: _____

Failure: _____

Lesson: _____

Saving is essential to achieving Superhero Success™, and self-control is vital for accomplishing this. List three things you can do to save more personal time, save more personal energy, and save more money in your life.

To save more personal time, I will:

1. _____
2. _____
3. _____

To save more personal energy, I will:

1. _____

2. _____

3. _____

To save more money, I will:

1. _____

2. _____

3. _____

Life is like your own personal bank. Everyone is given 86,400 seconds every single day of their lives to invest as they choose. There are no withdrawals, so if you don't invest them or spend them, you don't get them back. There is the possibility of earning interest, but only if you invest them wisely. What are your time investment habits? Are you earning interest on your time?

List three things you can do today to better organize your personal game plan for Superhero Success™. Achieving success is a mindset, but you MUST have an organized plan, along with the self-control to do all the little stuff necessary for its attainment.

1. _____

2. _____

3. _____

Building a lifestyle by design and living a life of your choosing is what Super-hero Success™ is all about. This Planner was not placed in this book for fun... it was placed to help you WIN - to help you break through the challenges you face and learn the skills needed to succeed at high levels in your job, or at your business, and more importantly at LIFE!

Gordy's character is more symbolic of the way we all *should* be in life: FEARLESS. Unfortunately, the villains of fear are very powerful and we all have to deal with them throughout our lives. It's our ability to face them head-on and keep them contained that determines the speed at which we all can achieve Superhero Success™.

You have the power to break through anything! Now go do it!

Get my FREE 14-day video training and ebook:
How To Become A Network Marketing Superhero And
Go From Part Time Income To Lifestyle Freedom
www.TWWalker.com

CAPE-ability® *GRID*

C HARACTER
Starts with accurate thinking about who you are, what you want, and what you stand for...

A TTITUDE
Is the seedling of outcome. It all comes from mindset...

P ERSEVERANCE
You must first define your fears in order to break through them...

E NTHUSIASM
Is the fuel that keeps you soaring high and far...

Having CAPE-ability® is a responsibility.
Accomplishment requires **Performance.**
Performance requires **Leadership**.
Leadership requires **Action** and **Attitude.**

— Message From The Author —

This book was never intended to change the world. It was only intended to provide you, the reader, with a fun, light-hearted story to help you remember what the important things are in life, and also to provide you with a little inspiration to propel you forward with your life and business.

Having a love of Superheroes, dating back to my childhood, I always felt like we have so much in common and so much to learn from them, and it seems I've always thought of one Superhero or another during various challenges I've encountered in my life. You can pretty much pick a challenge you've faced and there's some "super power" you probably wished you had at the time, right?

I've been fortunate to have failed and succeeded in many businesses over the years, but it was the dogged persistence and brilliance of the all the Superheroes I came to love as a kid that always remind me to keep pushing forward. Hopefully the same will happen for you after reading this book, whether you're a fan of Superheroes or not.

Although I intend to publish more books in the future as I continue my journey, this was the first for me. By following me on Facebook you will get to know 'The Man Behind The Cape' because unlike many Superheroes, I will not travel this journey alone. It's the amazing people I meet, work with, mastermind with, and grow with that I tend the learn the most from, so if you're in one of my many circles "Thank You" for being a part of this amazing journey with me.

I had such a great time writing this book, but it would not have become a realization for me if it had not been for something that happened in 2011 that seemed unfortunate at the time.

On July 29th , 2011 I was notified that my [then] fiancé [now wife] Heather had fallen while at work. It was serious. After being airlifted to a trauma center, she remained there for seven days unable to walk or function normally. She had suffered a traumatic brain injury, otherwise known as a TBI.

After seven days there, she was transferred to a rehabilitation hospital, where she spent the next four weeks going through intense physical and cognitive therapies just to regain basic physical and motor skills. Upon being released, I was charged with her care since I have a home office. There was no timetable for her recovery, or if she would have a complete one. Exactly ten days later, I was driving her back from a treatment she was receiving from a local acupuncturist when the unthinkable happened: at 45 mph, a truck illegally turned in front of us and we collided. Within minutes, paramedics were on the scene. Our vehicle was nearly totaled, and we were taken away by ambulance to a local hospital. There, she was diagnosed with a second TBI, and nearly all progress she had made, was gone. I suff ered a broken foot and also required back surgery.

The next several months were very trying for both of us as we fought to regain our former physical and mental selves, but it was during this time that we made the conscious decision that changes needed to happen; in my businesses and in our lives. And we did. Together, we joined hearts and hands and said, "We're going to get through this and be stronger because of it!" She said words to me that still resonate with me today, "I believe it!" We realized that life was too short to not do what you really want to do and live life to the fullest extent humanly possible.

The consulting company I had built from the ground up in 2000 immediately took a back seat because of all my realizations, and I began a full time conversion of my entire business model to online, so I could travel when I wanted versus when my clients needed me to.

Because of what we'd been through I made the decision to turn a corner in my professional life and create more residual income so we would be prepared the next time big challenges arrived in our lives. This is when I started my blog at www.TWWalker.com where I share stories, lessons, advice, motivation, and inspiration about starting a home business - helping people with a strong desire to succeed and create a lifestyle that provides real freedom.

Everything I do revolves around helping people live better!

I married Heather a short 7 months after the second accident in a lovely beach ceremony where she accomplished one of the major goals she set for herself while still in a wheelchair, when we decided that life was not going to stop us from charging forward: she walked down the sandy aisle unassisted. Although there's still a long road ahead for my wife, she has been one of my biggest inspirations. Most importantly, she has solidified in me what it really means to be a Superhero.

— About The Author —

TW Walker is an entrepreneur with unmatched vision, sharp wit, and keen sense of humor. He attributes this to being stuffed in a stocking that was too small when he was born (Christmas Baby), and also being dropped on his head multiple times as a child.

He unknowingly began his quest for "Superherodom" at the early age of three, when he was openly struck by a speeding car and not expected to see another day. But he was a Superhero in the making. Donning a full body cast instead of a cape for the next nine months of rehabilitation and recuperation, he was forced to use his imagination instead of his legs to play. He never lost this ability to use his imagination from that day forward.

TW learned the value of carving his own path by renting out his Big Wheel that he could no longer use because of his injuries. An entrepreneur was born. Never losing sight of the "child within", he crafted and published his first comic strip in his early twenties about a wacky Superhero, and purchased his first "real" business. Today, as the author and co-author of several books, including a best seller with world-renowned motivational, business, and leadership experts Tony Robbins, Wayne Dyer, and Brian Tracy, he coaches success-minded people on how to create residual income and succeed in network marketing without altering an already busy schedule most entrepreneurs have.

As veteran of high level small business consulting he teaches other entrepreneurs and small business owners how to achieve Superhero Success™ in life and business by mastering simple principles, systems, and processes... and not taking life too seriously. TW encourages others to avoid running into the same walls over and over again. He does confess, however, that this is considerably easier if you HAVE been dropped on your head as a child.

With his humorous approach to some of the most daunting obstacles people face in life, he reminds audiences of all ages that the sleeping super powers lying within each of us to achieve success are ready to be awoken.

His philosophy is to live a lifestyle of design, rather than default and he shows people how to do this by expanding CAPE-ability® to break through fears that debilitate growth. Known to wear a cape and tights at times, with his humorous approach to some of the most daunting obstacles people face in life and in their businesses, he reminds people of all ages that the sleeping super powers lying within them to achieve success are ready to be awoken. He also reminds them of just how valuable falling on your face can be.

TW lives in a secluded, private lair on the southwest coast of Florida with his wife Heather, and their "real" white fluffy dog, Jack.

— Praise For TW Walker's Superhero Success —

"Superhero Success is a must-read for anyone wanting an entertaining and empowering, yet easy to read book that will help unlock the superhero powers that often lie dormant within. I often say, "If somebody did it, that means it's possible for anybody, but God didn't just make you anybody; He made you somebody". Well, this book has that powerful theme all through it. In the words of Benjamin Franklin, "Empty your wallet into your mind, and your mind will fill your wallet". This book is a great investment, get it now and enjoy it as I have!"

Dr. Stan Harris, aka Dr. BreakThrough
Martial Artist, Minister, Motivational Speaker, Author

"Being in the fitness industry, I know many of the fears people face and also the monumental changes they experience once they break through them. Superhero Success illustrates this point so well with a fun story about a young boy, his dad, and a supercool Superhero! Great read for anyone looking for some inspiration and motivation to break through fear and succeed at anything."

Forrest Walden
CEO | IronTribe Fitness
Infusionsoft Marketer Of The Year

"Wow! Superhero Success is a powerhouse filled with nuggets of wisdom all done in an entertaining fashion through the power of story. Genius is making the complex simple. TW Walker has simplified complex success principles in a fun way that kids and adults of all ages can enjoy."

Eiji Morishita | CEO
Genius Squared
#1 Leader in Genius Generating Technologies

— Speaking —

TW Walker teaches people how to create a strong entrepreneurial mindset and is available for speaking engagements. He offers a unique and fresh approach that educates people on how to direct thoughts into physical reality. Audiences will be entertained with stories and humor through the clever use of metaphors and comic strip analogies in his presentations. **With his trademark Fear Sucks® mantra, audiences are left feeling inspired, motivated, and confident.** More importantly, audiences will learn the skills necessary to achieve Superhero Success™ in life and business by expanding their CAPE-ability® and conquering debilitating fears.

Primary Keynote Topics include:
- Conquering Fear
- Goal Achievement
- Leadership
- Peak Performance

TW is also available to speak at business events…

Primary Business Topics include:
- Self Promotion
- Social Media
- How To Build A Six Figure Income Online

Custom talks will be considered upon request.

"I feel truly blessed to be able to share my message in so many ways…If you or someone you know is looking for a speaker that knows how to motivate, inspire, and teach your audience how to think BIGGER and be MORE, all while keeping them laughing, then get in touch with me. You'll be glad you did."

Top 4 Reasons Event Coordinators Love Booking TW Walker:

1. An Empowering, Yet Humorous Message
Audiences will laugh and learn from TW's sarcastic, witty sense of humor about some of life's most daunting obstacles and challenges. They will be ready to strap on a cape after hearing the motivational lessons, powerful strategies, and humorous, entertaining stories.

2. Successful In Life And Business
Aside from his seminar/speaking business, TW has built multiple six figure businesses online, including a consulting business servicing clients all around the world, and has even found success in the brick and mortar world as a car wash owner. Now a home business consultant, he teaches entrepreneurs how to find, evaluate, and successfully build a network.

3. Superhero Credibility And Experience As A Speaker
TW is one of less than 100 people in the world to have his work endorsed by the Napoleon Hill foundation and is also recognized in Entrepreneur. He has collaborated with world renowned marketing experts Dan Kennedy, Bill Glazer, and has collaborated with New York Times Best Selling authors Tony Robbins, Brian Tracy, and Wayne Dyer.

4. Experience You Can Rely On
As the son of a Sam Walton disciple, TW learned all aspects of being a successful entrepreneur from his father who learned the skill directly from the godfather of retail before Wal-mart became a household name. He has provided private consultation to independent retailers around the world for more than a decade, speaking to groups of various sizes.

For booking fees and details, please contact:

Breakthrough Media Network
15 Paradise Plaza, Ste. 272
Sarasota, FL 34239

Email: booktw@twwalker.com
Web: www.TWWalker.com

If you found this book fun, entertaining, and inspiring, I'm sure it will have that effect on someone you know. We need more Superhero-minded people like you in the world, so please help develop more people like you and I and give a copy of this book to them. Without you, they may remain villains to fear and never find it.

Write down five people you will give a copy of this book to:

1.) _____

2.) _____

3.) _____

4.) _____

5.) _____

Thank you for investing your valuable time with me and the gang. I look forward to providing you more inspiration and entertainment…and helping you expand your CAPE-ability® to achieve Superhero Success™!

All My Best,

TW Walker

Get my FREE 14-day video training and ebook:
How To Become A Network Marketing Superhero And
Go From Part Time Income To Lifestyle Freedom
www.TWWalker.com

www.ingramcontent.com/pod-product-compliance
Lightning Source LLC
Chambersburg PA
CBHW071351090426
42738CB00012B/3080